THE THOTH TAROT:

Descriptions, Correspondences, Symbols, and Interpretations

Scott D. Miller, Ph.D.

ISBN 978-0-9966624-2-0

© 2017, Scott D. Miller

All rights reserved. No part of this book may be reproduced in any form without written permission of the authors.

Cover and Interior Design: Annabel Brandon

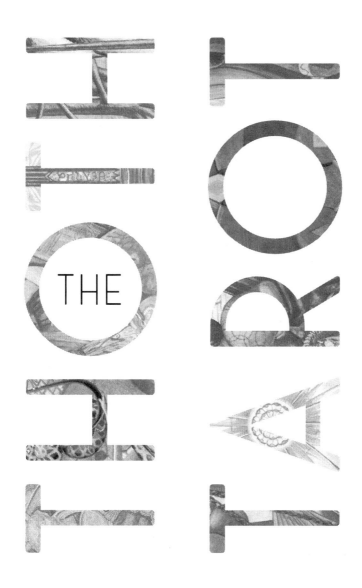

THE THOTH TAROT

SCOTT D. MILLER

CONTENTS

Introduction	3
Foreword	5
Card Overview	7
Astrology and the Tarot	11
The Qabala and the Tarot	15
Using the Tarot	21
The Major Arcana	25
The Minor Arcana	147
Wands	148
Cups	179
Swords	213
Disks	248
Bibliography	280

1: INTRODUCTION

The Tarot is much more than a colorful collection of occult symbols and arcane pictures. In today's world, a Tarot Deck is often relegated to a prop in supernatural thrillers or to the realm of psychics and fortunetellers.

But in reality its function is so very much more. From its origins in medieval times, it has, over the generations, slowly grown to encompass and organize much of what has grown to be called the "occult tradition." Although not scientific in today's sense, it has proven to be a collection of symbols and relationships that appeals to us human beings in a very direct and powerful manner. Few people, whether adept in its use or previously unfamiliar with these cards, remain unaffected when exposed to the mysteries within.

In this book, Scott has shared his personal and continuing voyage through the many ideas and concepts the Tarot presents – particularly in the THOTH deck. In the half century I've spent immersed in its lessons, I personally have seen and owned many of the world's finest decks, but the THOTH deck, to my mind at least, "has it all."

Many have attempted to systematize the concepts and relationships between differing approaches to "hidden wisdom" and I'm sure there will be many more in the years to come. In this book, Scott shares his own personal approach in great detail, employing not only the Tarot, but other approaches to enrich the Tarot's use, not only as a tool of divination, but as a "picture book of existence."

To make the Tarot of value, each person must undertake the journey in a personal, intimate manner, but one would be hard pressed to begin his or her journey with a better tour guide.

Bruce Bernstein
Chicago, IL

2: FOREWORD

"Do you believe in the paranormal?" the man asked me. When I replied, "No," he reached into a coat pocket, producing a Tarot deck. The cards were beautiful, dare I say works of art. I would later learn it was a very special deck, known as The Thoth Tarot. The captivating images were painted by Britsh artist Lady Frieda Harris under the direction of a person many consider the most influential practitioner of magick in history—person others either love or loathe, Aleister Crowley.

After shuffling the cards, he set them on the table and asked they be cut into four piles. From each, the top cards were removed and placed side by side in a row. "Ever had your cards read?" he asked. Once again, I answered, "No." Then he began, slowly moving from left to right, speaking about each in turn.

To say the experience was shocking does not do it justice. Disturbing, jarring, are far better words. Without going into the details, what the man told me that day was not only deeply personal, but also contained a breadth and level of detail known only to me or my immediate family.

Once my alarm subsided, it was replaced with a sense of intense curiosity combined with excitement. How did he do it? How did this man know so much given that we'd never met before? Somehow, within minutes, he created a profound feeling of familiarity and closeness, of being understood and seen.

Originally, I'd reached out to this person to help with a project a group of researchers and I were doing on top performing psychotherapists—a group that excels, in part, by engendering strong feelings of being heard and understood. We hoped to find clues to their success by investigating other disciplines in which relationship skills played a significant role. Little did I know at the time, just how much the magickal arts would offer to anyone wanting to understand and help both themselves and others.

Over a five-year period, I kept a journal. I made detailed notes of my visits with the man, who patiently guided my efforts to make sense of and do readings with the Tarot. Eventually, I organized my notes into searchable, electronic document. At the same time any and all material related the Thoth deck that I read in books or found online made it into the file. You hold that volume in your hands now.

I do not claim the material within is original or complete. In all likelihood, you will experience it as a bit schematic, with some parts more complete than others. Whatever the shortcomings, I hope it will prove helpful in your efforts to make sense and use of the Thoth Deck.

Scott D. Miller
Chicago, Illinois (USA)
www.scottdmiller.com

3: CARD OVERVIEW

The Tarot deck was originally a book of wisdom.

- 78 Total cards.
- 22 Major Arcana, called "Atu" or Keys:
  - Represent the cyclic pattern of birth, death, and rebirth that we experience throughout life;
  - Typically, give answers or messages regarding the question or situation at hand;
  - Generally, have an astrological sign, planetary or elemental symbol in the lower right of the card and a letter of the Hebrew alphabet on the left;
  - Together, they represent three major phases of our life:
    - The Fool represents the spark and subsequent journey;
    - Cards 1 (Magus) through 7 (Chariot) deal with finding a personal identity;
    - Cards 8 (Adjustment) through 15 (The Devil) have to do with withdrawing into ourselves and connecting deeply with our inner world;
    - Cards 16 (The Tower) through 22 (The Universe) relate to the reintegration of our spiritual essence and collective unity with all that exists.
- 16 Court cards:
  - Signify aspects of our own personality, qualities, talents, or abilities; or
  - Different personas or masks that we choose to wear when interacting with the world; and can also
  - Relate in some way to people who are important in our lives. Also show us what we have to learn and what we wish to master, as well as any special talents we have.

- Knight = Father
- Queen = Mother
- Prince = Idealistic
- Princess = Openness

- 40 Minor Arcana:
  - Represent a particular test, challenge or opportunity that feeds life with experience;
  - Concern the smaller, more direct lessons of life;
  - All range from 1 to 10:
    - 1 = The Spark, the Root, the Source, the Origin (Start)
    - 2 = Will, Attraction, Balance, Opposites (Interact)
    - 3 = Virtue, Abundance, Sorrow, Work (Productivity)
    - 4 = Completion, Luxury, Truce, Power (Results)
    - 5 = Strife, Disappointment, Defeat, Worry (Challenges)
    - 6 = Victory, Pleasure, Science, Success (Overcome)
    - 7 = Boldness, Debauchery, Futility, Failure (Excess)
    - 8 = Swiftness, Resignation, Interference, Prudence (Persistence)
    - 9 = Strength, Happiness, Cruelty, Gain (Stability)
    - 10 = Oppression, Satiety, Discontinuance, Wealth (End)

- The Court and Minor Arcana Cards come in four suits:
  - Wands = Will, desire, intent, passion (without tempering: arrogance, selfishness, ruthlessness);
  - Cups = Heart, understanding, feelings, perception, intuition (without surrender to a higher purpose: self-delusion, self-indulgence);
  - Swords = Mind, reason, intellect, judgment, analysis, communication (without objectivity: dogmatic, indecisive, conflict);
  - Disks = Matter, physical reality (family, career, health, finances), integrity, loyalty, pragmatism (without flexibility: dullness, pessimism, stubbornness);

But the Tarot recognizes numbers as spiritual symbols or the portals of initiation into each distinct stage of life. Master numbers are from 0 to 10 (also known as the decade). A reading can be done using the key words below in combination with the suit of the card (wands, disks, swords, and cups):

- 0 = Nothingness, potential;
- 1 = Unity, divine spirit (eternal masculine principle), independence, new starts, explosion of energy;
- 2 = Duality, divine receptivity (eternal feminine principle), balance, harmony, a partnership, cooperation with others;
- 3 = Divine intelligence (eternal principle of neutrality), creative self-expression, communication;
- 4 = Stability, hard work, physical manifestation, pause to think and reflect, limitations;
- 5 = Disruption, variety (good and bad), ups and downs, freedom but progress;
- 6 = Equilibrium, balance restored, love, responsibility, service;
- 7 = Expansion, understanding, faith, introspection, wisdom;
- 8 = Stability through change, power attainment, material satisfaction;
- 9 = Foundation and completion, humanitarianism, tolerance;
- 10 = Form, transition, something ends, something begins.

4: ASTROLOGY AND THE TAROT

- A deeper reading of the cards is possible when integrated with an understanding of the planet and sun signs:
  - The Major Arcana have 12 sun signs and 10 planets.
  - The Minor Arcana show the sun sign with a particular planet in that sign.
- Planets symbolize the primary energy, the type of energy being released:
  - Sun = (Fire) Extroverted. Courage, active, illuminates and reveals, optimism, generous, visible. Can cause burns or loss of contact with inner-self thereby risking becoming superficial, dogmatic, and authoritarian.
  - Moon = (Water) Introverted. Passive, receptive, helps you see in the dark (supports intuition). Rules imagination, fantasy life, and dream world. Can cause illusions as it casts shadows that hide the road ahead and distort reason.
  - Mercury = (Air) Swiftness. Lively, mercurial, power of transmission (talk, write, learn, teach). A liability for someone who holds onto information instead of integrating it as the pace will lead to feeling overwhelmed and frustrated. A state of conflict, struggle, and futility follows.
  - Venus = (Water) Harmonious. Peace, beauty, sensitivity, mood swings. Provides social grace and elegance but also can contribute to vanity and emotionalism.
  - Mars = (Fire) Assertive. Ambition and initiative. Always pushing the limits of possibility. Rules new beginnings and generates the heat of passion, enterprise, and courage. Can be aggressive and destructive as well as helpful.
  - Jupiter = (Fire) Expansive. Dynamic, bigger than life. The planet of faith, perseverance, and enthusiasm. Its benevolence can be a problem as it gives whatever is asked for in supersized portions.
  - Saturn = (Earth) Challenging. Tradition, convention, stability. Father Time, the disciplinarian who sets limits and time constraints. Delivers self-respect for a job well done, but ruthless when it isn't.

- Uranus = (Air) Freedom. Unaffected by dogma and prejudice. Higher mind. Brings hidden knowledge to the surface, evoking powerful change.
- Neptune = (Water) Intuitive. Divine compassion. The mystical word, beyond words.
- Pluto = (Water). Transformation, transcendence, revitalization. Bringing the deepest feelings to the surface.

- The constellations (Zodiac) express how the energy is manifested:
  - 1. Aries (March 21 - April 20) FIRE (Sun) = Me first, the will to be, pushing through obstacles (ram), when blocked can go from open and good natured to sullen and insensitive, The Emperor.
  - 2. Taurus (April 21 - May 21) EARTH (Venus) = Slow and steady, creator of structure and form, determined and tenacious, avoids conflict unless backed into a corner, can be stubborn, lethargic, and greedy, The Hierophant.
  - 3. Gemini (May 22 - June 21) AIR (Mercury) = Appetite for information, main question is, "why?" Embraces duality, union of opposites. Can be indecisive, confused, and unreliable, The Lovers.
  - 4. Cancer (June 22 – July 23) WATER (Moon) = Ocean of receptivity, Mother of the Zodiac, keeps everything within itself, feels emotionally exposed and vulnerable unless on familiar turf, withdraws when insecure, can be overly sensitive and defensive when feeling at risk, The Chariot.
  - 5. Leo (July 24 – August 23) FIRE (Sun) = Fire of creativity, Father of the Zodiac, protector, strong, romantic, outgoing, warm, passionate, and charismatic, commands attention. When opposed, can become morose, cynical, and tyrannical, Lust.
  - 6. Virgo (August 24 – September 23) EARTH (Mercury) = Gathering and analysis of information, service. Can be overly critical and have low self-esteem, The Hermit.
  - 7. Libra (September 24 – October 23) AIR (Venus) = Balance, harmony, equilibrium, charm and grace. When out of balance, can be superficial and indecisive, Adjustment.
  - 8. Scorpio (October 24 – November 22) Water (Pluto and Mars) = Transition, constant state of transformation, deep, intense passion,

pursuit of self-knowledge, the scorpion is the lowest level of awareness (followed by a phoenix, and an eagle) and can, if pressed too much, deliver a sting to others or self, Death.

- 9. Sagittarius (November 23 – December 21) FIRE (Jupiter) = Expansion, fully engaged in every experience, perceptive, time to take risks, philosophical and idealistic. If constrained, can fire poison arrows at others or self, Art.

- 10. Capricorn (December 22 – January 20) EARTH (Saturn) = Duty bound, strong sense of purpose, goal-directed, tenacious and sure-footed. Strong sense of propriety and self-protection and can keep emotions inside. Carelessness and disorganization results when energy is blocked, The Devil.

- 11. Aquarius = (January 21 – February 19) AIR (Saturn [limitation] and Uranus [liberation]) = "I know" stance, forward thinking and inventive, crusader of ideas, seeking liberation, can be brutally insensitive, The Star.

- 12. Pisces, the last sign (February 20 – March 20) WATER (Neptune) = Closest to spirit, divine level of compassion, mystic, seer, psychic, can be enmeshed and invasive, The Moon.

- Sun signs are divided into:
  - Positive (outgoing, strong, and active: Aries, Gemini, Leo, Libra, Sagittarius, and Aquarius) and Receptive (internalizing, nurturing, tenacious: Taurus, Cancer, Virgo, Scorpio, Capricorn, and Pisces);
  - Cardinal (Initiation: Aries, Cancer, Libra, Capricorn), Fixed (Stability: Taurus, Leo, Scorpio, Aquarius), and Mutable (Adaptability: Gemini, Virgo, Sagittarius, Pisces).

5: THE QABALA AND THE TAROT

The Qabalah is an ancient Jewish mystical system that teaches that all life (animal, plant, mineral)—everything that was, is or will be—comes from One Universal Source. We all share the same energy and destiny.

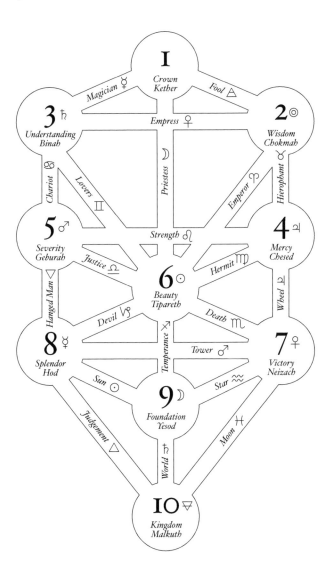

The "Tree of Life" contains 10 divine attributes of consciousness, called the Sephiroth. It is a schematic of how to live our lives as self-realized beings. A fully realized human life embodies all of the attributes.

Together, Kether, Binah, and Chokmah create the Supernal Triangle, or Holy Trinity, forming the basis for our journey into physical manifestation.

The Qabalah also depicts existence of Four Worlds—four distinct levels of reality represented in Tarot by the four suits:

- Atziluth (FIRE, wands): Nearest to divine wisdom, called the world of emanations, the field of potentiality (thought, inspiration, will). KETHER.

- Briah (WATER, cups): World of creation, transcendant awareness (inner spirit, intuition, understanding, and wisdom). BINAH and CHOKMAH.

- Yetzirah (AIR, swords): Formative world (higher mind, intellect nurturing potential manifestations). CHESED-GEBURAH-TRIPARETH-NETZACH-HOD-YESOD.

- Assiah (EARTH, disks): Physical world (matter, action-reaction). MALKUTH.

The last world is special and important as the physical realm is where we are able to actually see the laws of manifestation in effect. However, because we are unaware of our complete, true nature, we are unable to exercise our potential as conscious co-creators of the world. We end up acting in accordance with the programming of our culture, families, and peers.

It is the work of the Qabalah, and Tarot, to remind us of our grandeur and illuminate our path, pointing the way out of the darkness (reactive level) and into the Light (proactive level). In truth, the process is a kind of remembrance. Falling into the physical plane, we live in a cloud of uncertainty, having forgotten the nature of our true Self. Remembering what we are a part of—and that is everything—we naturally, consciously ascend the path shown on the Tree of Life.

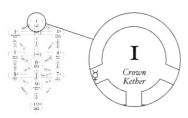

Position on TOL:	Eternal, Spiritual perfection, Pure being Unity of number one, pureness of number one, however, just ideas, nothing yet formed, the point (the "no-thing" from which everything is possible). World of Atziluth
Element:	Fire
Cards:	Aces

Ace of wands = pureness of fire, the flame of an idea
Ace of cups = pureness of water, the source or the spring
Ace of swords = pureness of air, first wind of wind
Ace of disks = pureness of earth, first sprout of a tree

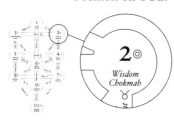

Position on TOL:	Creation, energy, wisdom Male potency (eternal masculine principle), the line Union of number two, balance and interaction of opposites, power of creation, and the first manifestation after the pure idea of ACE. World of Briah
Element:	Water
Cards:	Twos, Knights

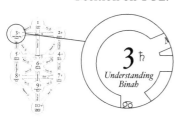

Position on TOL:	Understanding, realization, perception Female potency (enteral feminine principle), two dimensional. Manifestation of matter, World of Binah
Element:	Water
Cards:	Threes, Queens

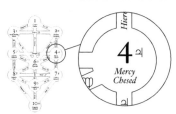

Position on TOL:	Mercy (kindness), condensation, the power of growth and stability
	Three-dimensional, solid body
	The beginning of the manifestation, of human consciousness, the intellectual mind
Element:	Air
Cards:	Fours

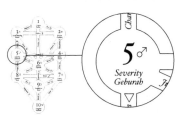

Position on TOL:	Severity, movement and change, destruction
	Counterbalance to Chesed, sorting out the excess, obsolete, and redundant
Element:	Air
Cards:	Fives

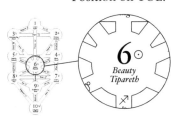

Position on TOL:	Beauty, consciousness and harmony, balance of the middle, mildness, and higher purpose
	Completes the "ethical triangle," standing for the principle of analysis, which includes: Chesed (Mercy), Geburah (Severity), Tipareth (Beauty)
Element:	Air
Cards:	Sixes, Princes

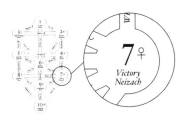

Position on TOL:	Victory, creativity and anarchy, sensitivity, uncontrolled instinct (force), wavering Part of the "Astral Triangle," sphere of illusion
Element:	Air
Cards:	Sevens

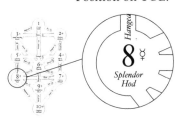

Position on TOL:	Splendor, intellect, logic, and structure (form), conscious mind, well thought structure (therefore restriction) Part of the "Astral Triangle," balancing Netzach (number 7), and sphere of Magick
Element:	Air
Cards:	Eights

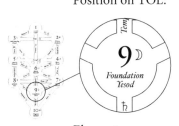

Position on TOL:	Foundation, reflection and imagination (moon and water) The balance point of the "Astral Triangle"
Element:	Air
Cards:	Nines

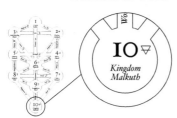

Position on TOL:	The root, the origin, the subconscious, kingdom, grounded, realm of life, physical beauty
Element:	Earth
Cards:	Tens, Princesses

6: USING THE TAROT

Just as we use a mirror to observe our exterior, we can use the images of the Tarot to approach (reflect) our inner reality. A mirror reflects reality without judging it.

MIXING THE CARDS:

- First, shake hands briefly (to relax any tension)
- Use the left hand, the one related to the unconscious and intuitive side of the brain
- Mix the fire, earth, air and water cards
- Cut into four piles, representing the four elements
- Tell the meaning of each element (fire = will; water = emotion; air = intellect/ideas earth = when combined with the other three, the final result)

ASK, "DO YOU HAVE A SPECIFIC QUESTION…"

- Most questions revolve around: Love, Health, and Money.
- "I can do a more general reading but…"

    "People often have a question…"
    "Generally, they develop questions during the reading…"
    "It will save a lot of time if you have a specific question…"

TRANSLATING THE CHOSEN CARDS:

- Pay attention to your first spontaneous reaction
- Use your intuition:

    "I can interpret the symbols and often get impressions. You have to let me know if we're on the right track…"

- Point to the picture and highlight images, colors, symbols. While doing so, take time to observe the person whose cards are being read.
- Look for patterns (e.g., a high proportion of a suit, number, astrological sign, or element).

PREDOMINANCE OF SUITS:

- *Wands*: More than likely dealing with the will and intent to create something new in life.
- *Cups*: Feelings and intuitions are making themselves known and require immediate attention.
- *Swords*: Pre-occupied with mind. Mental powers focused on analyzing the situation, integrating the information and ironing out any mental conflicts.
- *Disks*: Focus is on the mundane, day-to-day life.

PREDOMINANCE OF NUMBERS:

- *Aces*: experiencing an explosion of energy as raw potential begins its journey toward manifestation.
- *Twos*: Becoming aware of one's will and intent.
- *Threes*: Creative, formative energy is being generated in the situation.
- *Fours*: The core energy is taking form as it moves into physical manifestation.
- *Fives*: Disruption is occurring, but it will lead to further progress eventually.
- *Sixes*: Balance has been restored.
- *Sevens*: The desire for expansion is renewed.
- *Eights*: Changes are occurring which will ultimately help things stabilize.
- *Nines*: Here is the foundation upon which everything is built.
- *Tens*: The situation is completely locked into its physical manifestation.

PREDOMINANCE OF ASTROLOGICAL SYMBOLISM:

- *Aries*: The stage is set to take the initiative and just do it.
- *Taurus*: View the situation through the lens of convention, stability, and determination.
- *Gemini*: Take care to consider all aspects of the matter at hand.
- *Cancer*: Here the concern is with nurturing your feelings and expressing them.
- *Leo*: Focus on your strengths and protect your boundaries.
- *Virgo*: New information calls for careful analysis and judicious integration.
- *Libra*: Equilibrium and harmony are the ruling factors.
- *Scorpio*: Transitions are the focus, roll with them.
- *Sagittarius*: Take more risks, and your life expands.
- *Capricorn*: A strong sense of purpose dominates matters.
- *Aquarius*: Liberation is the overriding aspect.
- *Pisces*: The focus is one empathy and compassion.

PREDOMINANCE OF ELEMENTS:

- *Fire*: Become more in tune with internal desires and passions. Be bold and energetic.
- *Water*: Be receptive to feelings and intuition.
- *Air*: Analyze, synthesize, and integrate the facts. Be more communicative.
- *Earth*: Attend to finances, relationships, career, and family.
- Although rare, sometimes the cards do not make sense or shed light on the situation. In such instances, the person is being asked to rely on their conscious judgment.

7: THE MAJOR ARCANA

0. THE FOOL

TAROTNYMS

Planning/beginning/starting new project versus lack of follow through/results

Idealism versus useless daydreaming

Hope/optimism versus unrealistic/impractical

Openness/trusting versus lack of direction/commitment/naive

ONE'S BIRTH/BEGINNING

SNAPSHOT

INNOCENCE/FAITH/ENTHUSIASM/IDEALISM

BAUTA "HIDING PLACE" QUADRANT (SCOTT GROSSBERG):

The Mask: Innocence/Idealism	The Beast: Careless
What makes me who I am; How I view myself; What I'm attracted to; What I take for granted in myself.	How others view me; What I excuse in myself; My deepest urge; What I resort to under stress.
The Shadow: Plodding	The Light: Carefull
The thing I have no wish to be; What I think I've left behind; What I become when all else fails; What I still must learn to control.	What others think I need; What I look at with wonder; What I need for balance; What I desire to accomplish.

MEANING:

The Fool believes deep down that s/he is the selector of his/her own destiny, aimed at fun, love, and knowledge. The Fool is often thought of by others to be, and certainly becomes, careless when under stress. When pushed, the Fool becomes downright leaden in his/her ability to make any choice at all, not altogether indecisive but slow enough to act to sacrifice self-sufficiency.

Main Summary: Innocence, blind faith, open to experience, enthusiasm, action, starting a new venture.

Bottom Line Interpretations (Tarantino): Curiosity, spontaneity, and a spirit of adventure will lead you toward success. When people say it can't be done, show them how wrong they are by doing it. Negative: You have made some foolish choices lately. If you want to realize your goals, keep your commitments—pay attention to details and complete what you start.

CORRESPONDENCES:

(A method of assigning meaning and interdependent connections to the various aspects of the visible and invisible worlds wherein each color, sound, metal, plant, animal, organs of the human body, or anything in the material world, is said to have its origin in the invisible through specific energetic signatures).

- *Number*: 0, formless, potential
- *Hebrew*: 1, Aleph (The first of three mother letters [incl, Mem and Shin]), ⟨glyph⟩, Ox
- *Positive*: The positive break up of structures and limitations, selfless idealism, endless fantasy, optimism, trust to instincts
- *Negative*: The negative loss of structures, lack of responsiveness, useless daydreaming, infantalism
- *Planet*: Uranus (freedom, liberation)
- *Zodiac*: Aquarius (freedom through discipline)
- *Element*: Air
- *Tree of Life*: Kether (Crown/external/perfection) going to Chokmah (Energy/creation)
- *Color*: Yellow
- *Life Themes* (Scott Grossberg):
- "I am the sum of all my adventures"
  "And they shall know me by the choices I make"
- *Basic Divinatory Meaning* (Instruction booklet): In spiritual matters, represents ideas, thoughts, spirituality, that which endeavors to transcend earth. In material matters may show, if ill-dignified, folly, eccentricity, even mania. It represents the original, subtle, and sudden impulse coming from a strange and unexpected quarter. (Webster): The card represents the start of a journey. It is a sign of fresh starts and a new beginning.
- *Advice*: Take things as they are. Matters are proceeding as planned. Do your part to settle outstanding disagreements. Kill others with kindness and let them suffer the consequences of their actions. This is a good time to build your investments or remodel your home. Alternately: schedules are full,

time is at a premium. Take time to enjoy life's pleasures. Postpone business decisions temporarily. Use distraction and patience.

SYMBOLISM:

- The Fool is the symbol of true innocence, a perfect state of joy and freedom, the sure feeling to be one with the spirit of life, at any time;
- Green man represents springtime energy renewal;
- Horns, grapes, and sun disk on his belt represent a lust for life;
- Facial expression is one of divine madness;
- The crystal in his hand indicates that he is a visionary;
- The boots point outwards, showing that he has no direct contact with earth (pragmatic concerns/reality);
- The Fool has the number 0, for someone ready to go in any direction, open to all possibilities:
  - In Arabic letters the 0 has the shape of an egg, the symbol for the origin of life.
- The Fool is shown with an animal, as a symbol of nature, the animal soul is in perfect harmony with the spirit that just follows its instincts;
- The dove is a symbol of unconditional love;
- The butterfly represents metamorphisis;
- The tiger indicates either fearlessness or the "bite of reality;"
- The four circles represent creativity and regeneration at all levels;
- The rainbow is a symbol of integration.

INTERPRETATION:

The Fool is change, motion and the readiness to jump into life, with no cares ever.

The Fool knows no difference between possibility and reality, the zero means a total lack of hope and fear, the Fool suspects and plans nothing. He reacts directly to the current situation, nothing is calculated, and nothing is hidden.

He belongs nowhere, has no past, but an infinite future. Every moment is a new beginning.

The Fool is courage, optimism and the belief in life and himself. When times are hard, and we suffer the pressure of "being reasonable" or denying our instincts, the Fool reminds us that our inner person knows best what to do. "Always trust your instincts."

The Fool card in a Tarot deck is one of the most **mysterious, and perhaps disturbing,** of all the Tarot cards. Its many meanings, although superficially obvious, eludes concrete definition. It can mean many different things both within a Tarot reading and without; just when you think you have its meaning nailed, events conspire to show you the foolishness of that conclusion.

Below are seven different and sometimes contradictory meanings to help you understand the Fool, not just in a Tarot reading, but to understand the Fool within us.

1. A simpleton or Bodhisattva? Historically, the Fool card was unnumbered, although there were exceptions and one of them was to number the Fool as either zero or twenty-two. By not assigning a number to the Fool, we are effectively placing it outside the pack of Tarot cards. We are saying that he lives outside the world, outside society and outside of the rules governing all phenomena.

As observers of the Fool, safe behind all our experiences, all those experiences that have destroyed our innocence, like holding us in a walled city; we gaze out upon the Fool and we conclude, this is a madman, a simpleton; look how he acts–like such a Fool.

However there may be some who disagree, who mutter under their breath for they are afraid, experienced as they are, of who might hear; this is someone with **great spiritual awareness**; a Bodhisattva come out of great compassion for he has renounced nirvana to save all sentient beings. It would be a mistake to see this as foolish; he is no Fool, but a great man!

> The nature of the Bodhisattva is apparent from a teaching story in which three people are walking through a desert. Parched and thirsty, they spy a high wall ahead. They approach and circumnavigate it, but it has no entrance or doorway. One climbs upon the shoulders of the others, looks inside, yells "Eureka" and jumps over. The second then climbs up and repeats the actions of the first. The third laboriously

climbs the wall without assistance and sees a lush garden inside the wall. It has cooling water, trees, fruit, etc. But instead of jumping into the garden, the third person goes back out into the desert and seeks desert wanderers to tell them about the garden and how to find it. The third person is the Bodhisattva.

2. The most powerful of all the Trumps: the Fool is unnumbered, and without a number the Fool is free to travel wherever he wills, not constrained by traditional boundaries and being beyond the rules of law, his wanderlust can end up destabilizing the establishment. In almost all ways the Fool serves no real purpose in a Tarot deck, or a pack of playing cards for that matter. Does the Fool upset our ordered and balanced Tarot readings? Why have we kept him around?

3. The Fool is easy to overlook: It's easy to overlook the Fool, much like the court Jester in the Royal house. Although the court jester served no obvious purpose, it was this lack of purpose which gave the Jester so much power within the politics of the time. Able to mingle between different groups of people, he served as an excellent spy and in some sense, held power equal to the King or Queen; certainly this person was not someone to underestimate.

4. The Fool as zero: Zero indicates a divinity of absence; this is in contrast to the 'divinity of presence' which we are used to dealing with and thinking about (religion or defined routes of spirituality would be examples). The Fool indicates a place that lies beyond the command of language; a place where all contradictions are united; a place of "emptiness" a place where knowledge becomes ignorance or when the events of history are forgotten but the remains of those events are present all around us. Ultimately, the Fool represents that irrational idea that something can come from no-thing and in this sense, the whole of the Universe issued forth from the Fool.

5. The Symbol of Zero: Zero is a numerical sign which derives its meaning from the Arabic word *sifra* (cipher). It has no value of its own and replaces the values missing in other numbers. In this sense it represents objects which have no properties of their own, but rather it confers properties upon other objects. Zero, in connection with the Fool card, represents the initiatory aspect of the card; being unnumbered it may either validate or annul other cards depending on its position.

6. The Fool goes forward: In most depictions of the Fool, although there are exceptions, the Fool is moving forward. It represents action, movement, going forward and, based on the images, in one definite direction. The overcoming of fears, taking risks and confronting the unknown are all traits that are portrayed in the Fool. Inexperience doesn't hold the Fool back; innocence is what allows the Fool to move forward.

7. The Fool as innocence: There are many myths that are connected to the Fool. Most, such as Percivale, who wins the Holy Grail through his innocence and lack of experience; or Hoor-Pa-Kraat, the Egyptian lord of silence, who tread upon the crocodile god Sebek, the Devourer. Both indicate a quality of the Fool card that is difficult to understand. In the most abstract sense, if the Fool was to ever have a single thought in his head, he would no longer be innocent, rather he would be experienced. Thoughts destroy innocence. The connection that the madman, the simpleton and the Fool have to divinity is in their innocence; their lack of rational thoughts–their lack of politics and their "empty headedness." It is their innocence which makes them appear, to rational human beings, as foolish.

DIVINATION:

You are ready for a new beginning, perhaps a quantum leap. Give in, dare to leap, even if fear attempts to hold you back. Trust the voice from within your heart.

Question to ponder: What is the "tiger of fear" for you? How do you imagine the courageous leap into the new? What does it look like? Where does your heart call you to go?

Affirmation to give yourself: I now follow my heart. I am open and ready to go wherever it may lead me.

I. THE MAGUS (MAGICIAN/JUGGLER)

TAROTNYMS

Skillful, brilliant and assertive versus aggressive/arrogant

Initiative versus impulsive/superficial

Pioneering versus impractical/egotistical/lonely

LUCKY/GIFTED VERSUS SUPERFICIAL/SELFISH/GIVE UP EASILY WHEN DIFFICULTIES COME YOUR WAY

SNAPSHOT

ONE'S THOUGHTS/MENTAL STATE ADOLESCENCE/SELF-ASSURANCE/WILL TO ACT (ASSERTIVENESS/ACTIVITY)/MASTERY

BAUTA "HIDING PLACE" QUADRANT (SCOTT GROSSBERG):

The Mask: Wilful & Skillful What makes me who I am; How I view myself; What I'm attracted to; What I take for granted in myself.	The Beast: Manipulating How others view me; What I excuse in myself; My deepest urge; What I resort to under stress.
The Shadow: Frivolous/uncaring/removed The thing I have no wish to be; What I think I've left behind; What I become when all else fails; What I still must learn to control.	The Light: Whimsy/playfulness What others think I need; What I look at with wonder; What I need for balance; What I desire to accomplish.

MEANING:

The Magician is the creator, manipulator, transformer, the one who wants something more. The Magician believes that if s/he applies will, it will happen. Others experience the Magician as manipulative, and when stressed becomes so in an effort to achieve his/her aims. When failing to make some gratifying breakthrough, the Magician can/will lash out at self, and when backed into a corner, will remove him/herself aesthetically and emotionally, thereby appearing to others as uncaring.

Main Summary: Fast, pioneering, innovative, adaptive, self-assured, sixth sense, intellectual need for understanding and control, self-realization, activity, focus, initiative.

Bottom Line Interpretations (Tarantino): Stay focused on the outcome you want to achieve but don't get hung up on just one way of doing things. You may have to revise your plans several times before you reach your goal, but when all is said and done, you will succeed. Negative: You create what you imagine; therefore, think positively and then act creatively.

CORRESPONDENCES:

- *Number*: 1, innate, primal
- *Hebrew*: 2, Bet, ב, House
- *Positive*: Initiator, pioneer, leadership, courage, individualism
- *Negative*: Dominating, impulsive, egotistic, boastful, willful, aggressive
- *Planet*: Mercury. Fast, intelligent (according to Wikipedia, Mercury is the messenger of the gods, guide of the dead and protector of merchants, shepherds, gamblers, liars, and thieves)
- *Element*: Air—success through adaptability in combination with endurance
- *Tree of Life*: Binah (realization/understanding)-Kether (Crown/eternal/spiritual/perfection)
- *Animal*: Ibis, ape
- *Magickal Tools*: Wand, caduceus (Wikipedia indicates it is a recognized symbol of commerce and negotiation, two realms in which balanced exchange and reciprocity are recognized as ideals. The caduceus is also used as a symbol representing printing, again by extension of the attributes of Mercury (in this case associated with writing and eloquence). Medicine, especially in the US, have inappropriately used the caduceus as a symbol. The correct symbol for medicine is the Rod of Asclepius, depicted as a single serpent entwined rod, associated with a Greek god of the same name (which was associated with healing)
- *Scent*: Mastic, storax
- *Consciousness*: Attention, self-consciousness
- *Life Themes*:
- "I am the sum total of all my creations."
  "And they shall know me by the stories I tell."
- *Basic Divinatory Meaning*: (instruction booklet) Skill, wisdom, adroitness, elasticity, craft, cunning, deceit, theft. Sometimes occult wisdom or power. Messages, business transactions. Ill-dignified: learning or intelligence interfering with the matter in hand. (Webster): Signifies the start of something new and important. This card provides an opportunity for the person to use his or her developed skills and move forward.

- *Advice:* Now is the time to stretch yourself and test your limits. Be adventurous, daring, and competitive—within limits. Success and recognition will follow. It's an excellent time to start new projects. Alternately: Pay attention to the rules and think twice before acting. Don't close yourself off from the help and guidance of others. Beware of arrogance. Make friends, not enemies.

INFLUENCES:

- *Mental*: Quick, sharp, alert, flexible, seizes opportunities, open to possibilities;
- *Emotional*: Emotional roller coaster, serendipitous, unpredictable;
- *Physical*: Flexible, lithe;
- *Spiritual*: Open to surrender, serves the Source, uses talents for the highest good.

SYMBOLISM:

- The Magus is also known as Mercury, messenger of the Gods. He is a master of communication and transformation. Oftentimes, Mercury balances on the line between white and black magick, and there's always a strong pull for him to satisfy the ego rather than offer himself up in service;
- The golden light that emanates from the Magus is a symbol of the light that flows through us when we live according to the maxim "As above, so below";
- His winged feet are a symbol of heavenly messages;
- The smile on his face is a symbol of optimism and the ability to convey his messages with a sense of humor;
- The fan above his head represents ever expanding awareness;
- His nakedness indicates he is open.

In the card, the Magus is juggling different objects that represent our ability to communicate and manifest in different areas of our lives:

- The coins represent manifesting material abundance and success in practical endeavors;

- Fire represents inspiration/transformation;
- The Ibis wand is a symbol of philosophy, religion and spirituality;
- The scroll represents the fine arts and written communication;
- The winged egg is a symbol of the psychic arts, inspired vision and spiritual transformation;
- The cup represents emotion;
- The snake represents regeneration;
- The sword is a symbol of analytical thinking, science and the intellect;
- The monkey represents flexibility/adaptability and is often found in paintings of Thoth, the Egyptian god of wisdom;
- The Caduceus from the Fool is also found in the Magus card. As the symbol is placed above the head of the Magus, its main meaning here is innovative thoughts;
- The lines in the background represent energy and lines of communication;
- The color blue represents mental energy; gold, flexibility, malleability; purple, divinity.

INTERPRETATION:

The Magus represents the will to create. He is able to help us keep our illusions intact.

In a reading can represent a person who seems to have "the Midas touch," who is multi-talented, gifted, and "lucky."

On a deeper more personal level, the Magus usually appears during a period when communication flows easily, and manifesting ideas seems to happen naturally or "as if by magick." You are now aware of your own giftedness but may find it difficult to maintain focus. If you do manage to stay with it, there is no limit to what you are able to achieve.

The Magician's shadow: Lack of self-esteem or willpower, magick used for selfish purposes, superficiality, egotism, condescendence, misuse of talents, lack of follow-through, trickster, theft.

Question to ponder: In what areas lie your talents? With what methods, and in what surroundings can you pass them on or share them?

Affirmation to give yourself: The full expression of my creative potential fulfills me and makes me happy and satisfied.

II. THE PRIESTESS

TAROTNYMS

The womb of life, receptivity, acceptance, versus being taken advantage of/doubts

Sensitivity versus overly so, unable to sense one's own needs

Patience/endurance versus passivity/self-sacrifice

Spiritual/feelings versus practical/reality/facts

ONE'S EMOTIONS/INTERNAL SENSE

SNAPSHOT

FERTILITY/MYSTERY/INTUITION/EVERYTHING THAT ELUDES THOUGHT AS A PATH TO UNDERSTANDING

BAUTA "HIDING PLACE" QUADRANT (SCOTT GROSSBERG):

The Mask: Intuition/Feelings What makes me who I am; How I view myself; What I'm attracted to; What I take for granted in myself.	The Beast: Unfathomable How others view me; What I excuse in myself; My deepest urge; What I resort to under stress.
The Shadow: Open book/Vengeful The thing I have no wish to be; What I think I've left behind; What I become when all else fails; What I still must learn to control.	The Light: Understandable What others think I need; What I look at with wonder; What I need for balance; What I desire to accomplish.

MEANING:

While the Magician performs his actions (miracles) openly, the Priestess waits, watches and works her magic invisibly, preferring less obvious actions and intentions. She is viewed by others as impossible to understand. When stressed, her actions become even more difficult to fathom. Pushed to the extreme, her quiet, behind the scenes machinations can surface and she becomes a blazing force to be reckoned with. To obtain balance, the Priestess should be more direct, forthcoming in her dealings with others.

Main Summary: Intuition, connection to the unconscious, awareness, patience, creative potential, seeing the potential, receptiveness, fertility, deep knowledge, spiritual knowledge, education, wisdom.

Bottom Line Interpretations (Tarantino): If you continue to seek advice from other people, you risk the chance of being misled. Trust your own intuition because at the moment, you are your best counsel. Negative: There's a lot more going on here than meets the eye. Before reaching a conclusion, take more time to learn about your situation.

CORRESPONDENCES:

- *Number*: 2, the symbol of duality

- *Positive*: Sensitivity, being one with the beginning of all, aware of the wisdom from the subconscious, intuitive knowledge, patience

- *Negative*: passivity at the wrong time, leading to weakness and a fear of life, changing moods, doubts, ignoring of reality

- *Planet*: Moon, representing all that is passive and receptive in human nature

- *Element*: Water

- *Hebrew letter*: 3, Gimel (Camel), ג

- *Tree of Life*: **Kether** (Crown/perfection/external) to **Tipheret** (Balance/harmony)

- *Archetype*: Maiden goddess, priestess, virgin

- *Complementary partner*: Magus (possessing all his skill and ability, but with far more insight and psychological mindedness. The Magus generates his own power, whereas the Priestess draws upon the forces of life itself).

- *Qabalistic worldview*: The path of Gimel between Tiphereth and Kether is the one that crosses the Abyss (often depicted as a desert)—a testing ground for the spiritual aspirant, where one faces inner demons and illusion. The Hebrew letter for Camel is appropriate here, since only a camel can carry somebody across the vast expanse of a desert.

- *Life Themes*:

    "I am the sum of all the secrets I keep."
    "And they will know me by my silence."

- *Basic Divinatory Meaning*: (instruction booklet) Pure, exalted, and gracious influence on matters, hence change, alternation, increase and decrease, fluctuation. May be lead away by enthusiasm unless careful balance is maintained. (Webster): The card represents wisdom, spiritual knowledge, and intuition. The person is entering a learning phase. His or her intuition is growing at this time.

- *Advice*: Trust your intuition more than your reason, act more on feelings than on facts. Take your time to think about your options. Tackle difficulties with enthusiasm—these are opportunities to learn. To be a winner now, don't withdraw. Alternately: you're expecting things to come to easily. Be careful not to give up right away when they don't. You're feeling a desire to escape, to withdraw into yourself. Shrug off your current lack of focus and work diligently to achieve your goals.

SYMBOLISM:

- She sits between two pillars, representing mercy and justice;
- Her naked, bare chest represents deep sensitivity;
- Her crown represent the world of vision and intuition to which she has access;
- The bow and arrow resting on her lap indicates that her information is direct from the source;
- The sea goggles indicate emotional perception;
- The veils suspended between them shows that it is the Priestess who allows us to penetrate the innermost secrets of life;
- The crystals represent the clarity of her perception on four levels: will, understanding, mind, and physicality;
- The camel represents self-sufficient;
- At the bottom of the card are shown nascent forms, fruits, symbolizing the beginning of life;
- The color white indicates purity; aqua blue, softness, peace; yellow/purple, spirit; green, creativity; pink, unconditional love.

INTERPRETATION

An indication that we are in communication with unseen forces. We must realize these unseen forces are greater than ourselves, and our ability to access this energy is a great responsibility. We must understand that we are all psychic, just as the Priestess. However, only those who respect the gift of psychic awareness and utilize the gifts and the knowledge beneficially acquire the noble presence and demeanor of the Priestess.

The Priestess rules our intuitive faculties. She helps us to see what is really in front of us, rather than seeing what appears to be there. She's a gentle and tranquil influence who can help us develop our inner psychic abilities.

As a symbol for deeper knowledge, the card can express a feeling of darkness, which might also be a feeling of fear, but also a feeling of beauty. We know there is more inside than we can see.

The best thing we can do is practice entering into the silence in order that we can 'hear' our intuition. Spend a little time in quiet contemplation, meditation, still the incessant chatter that is part of everyday life. This is something that so many of us don't make time to do often enough. As a result, we miss an enormous amount of information that we pick up through every waking hour, and store automatically.

Our ancient ability to read the signs of life still remains, whether we use it or not. But often we can be taken unawares by material reflecting.

DIVINATION:

You now have access to your intuitive powers. Develop them more fully. Guard your independence.

The person is entering a learning stage.

Questions to ponder: Ask yourself, "What is my hunch about this situation? Are there areas in your life in which you allow others to influence you rather than trusting your own intuition? What do I know about myself and this situation that I'm unwilling to face?"

Affirmation to give yourself: I trust my intuitive abilities

III. THE EMPRESS

TAROYNMS

Love, born responsible, caring, tolerance versus creating dependence

Devotion to others versus taking care of self

Emotion versus action

Seeking/creating unity versus standing on own

THE LOVE THAT SURROUNDS YOU

SNAPSHOT

MOTHER (DEVOTION PLUS PASSION)/TRUST/UNITY

BAUTA "HIDING PLACE" QUADRANT (SCOTT GROSSBERG):

The Mask: Protect & Comfort What makes me who I am; How I view myself; What I'm attracted to; What I take for granted in myself.	The Beast: Smothering How others view me; What I excuse in myself; My deepest urge; What I resort to under stress.
The Shadow: Uncaring The thing I have no wish to be; What I think I've left behind; What I become when all else fails; What I still must learn to control.	The Light: Distance What others think I need; What I look at with wonder; What I need for balance; What I desire to accomplish.

MEANING:

The Empress is the Great Mother, the eager protector with zealous encouragement. Those who nurture and protect are often viewed, even by those receiving of her comfort, as strangling and suffocating. When she feels under stress, she becomes repressing. Push her too far, and her defensive instincts make her suddenly and quickly withdrawn, unaffectionate and appear to be unloving.

Main Summary: Nurturing, security (safety) unconditional love, devotion, joining (unity of purpose [material and emotional]), creation (potential), deep emotion (unconscious), intuitive awareness, future-orientation.

Bottom Line Interpretations (Tarantino): Take a deep breath, slow down and relax. People want to help you if you just let them. Be gracious, delegate authority, and you'll get exactly what you want. Negative: Don't smother. If you want to succeed, stop trying to manipulate the circumstances and let the situation evolve at its own rate.

CORRESPONDENCES:

- *Number*: 3, the combination of the contrasts to a unity (synthesis, harmony)
- *Positive*: love, trust, fulfillment, the joy of great abundance
- *Negative*: Greed, envy, jealousy, laziness, dependence
- *Hebrew Letter*: 4, Daleth, ד, Door
- *Element*: Earth
- *Planet*: Venus (beauty, harmony, love)
- *Tree of Life*: From Chokmah (Energy/wisdom/creation) and Binah (undestanding)
- *Life Themes*:

    "I am the sum of what I protect."
    "And they will know me by the comfort I provide."

- *Basic Divinatory Meaning*: Love, beauty, happiness, pleasure, success, fruitfulness, good fortune, graciousness, elegance, gentleness. Ill-dignified: dissipation, debauchery, idleness, sensuality. (Webster): This card reveals someone who is loving, motherly, protective, and caring. It indicates a productive, emotionally stable period in the person's life.

- *Advice*: Express your ideas and take calculated risks. Getting what you want is your responsibility. Your passions are of primary importance to you now. News of a wedding, pregnancy or children. Alternately: Are you feeling inferior about your intellect, education, or communication skills? Stop it! Problems with your mother and other intimate women are imminent.

SYMBOLISM:

The Empress is the embodiment of all things feminine, giving life to the dreams of the Priestess and content to the vision of the Magus:

- The position of her hands indicates both the receiving and giving of love;
- The lotus in her right hand symbolizes the passive power of love;
- The crown of the Empress: Here again we see the unification of the sun and moon, meaning the energy with emotion. The Maltese cross emphasizes the unification of material and spiritual qualities;

- The face of the Empress: We see her looking toward the dove (holy), also to her left, toward the Emperor, and away from the sparrow (lustfulness);
- The pink and white pelican: Seen feeding it's young on its own blood. This symbolically shows the unconditional love that a mother uses to nourish her young with the very fiber of her being;
- The double-headed white eagle: (a similarity between the Emperor's red eagle) symbolically showing the result of unification of the different aspects of one's being;
- The moon and earth: The two are joined on this card and are surrounded by the forces of magnetism. The moon alludes to the emotional areas of the unconscious and the earth shows the manifestation, or realization, of those areas;
- The blue flames: These flames symbolize the minds comprehension of the "deeper things," the unconscious;
- The open archway: This can be seen as Heaven's Gate. What we see in the forefront is only a shadow of what lies behind, something infinitely more beautiful and wonderful;
- The red and white found on the card are symbolic of giving and receiving of love. The green is symbolic of creativity and fertility. Understanding and wisdom are represented here by the color blue.

INTERPRETATION:

The Empress is the friendlier, more approachable aspect of the female archetype. She stands for maternity, love and mercy; at the same time she's a symbol for sexuality and emotion. She is pure feeling, absolutely unintellectual, but basically life. The Empress is the Great Mother, representing the beginning of all life. She is the power of nature, causing change, renewal, major plans.

The Empress also stands for passion, a phase in which we cope with life on an emotional and joyful basis, rather than on the thoughtful. This could mean great satisfaction, but in an improper context, when actually more analysis is needed. The Empress can also stand for a reflective, emotional attitude, refusing to accept reality. It also could stand for a person who is greedy for joy and abundance when actually just more self-control is needed.

The Empress inspires you to listen to your dreams and visions, to protect and nurture them.

DIVINATION:

The beauty you see in others which attracts you to them is a beauty you carry within yourself. You are in the process of unfolding and evolving your femininity. This may be the right time to work through and clarify any mother-conflicts.

A productive, emotionally stable period in the person's life.

Questions to ponder: In your life is there a beautiful, strong woman from whom you would like to learn?

Affirmation to give yourself: I am filled with power and beauty.

IV. THE EMPEROR

TAROTNYMS

Authority but fair, fatherly, powerful versus hard to work with others/can be cruel if crossed

Willing to assume responsibility/lead/take on a new project versus lack of balance/joy in personal life/indecisiveness

Stability/order/status quo versus rule bound/unable to risk or take criticism

Rational/justice versus lacking feeling/mercy/attention to the individual

SNAPSHOT

The order that surrounds you

Father (authority/experience/provider)/order/security

BAUTA "HIDING PLACE" QUADRANT (SCOTT GROSSBERG):

The Mask: Leader/Father What makes me who I am; How I view myself; What I'm attracted to; What I take for granted in myself.	The Beast: Tyrannical How others view me; What I excuse in myself; My deepest urge; What I resort to under stress.
The Shadow: Slave The thing I have no wish to be; What I think I've left behind; What I become when all else fails; What I still must learn to control.	The Light: Cooperative What others think I need; What I look at with wonder; What I need for balance; What I desire to accomplish.

MEANING:

The Emperor is a leader, one who takes action as opposed to being passive. Those subject to his/her rules, or who feel the impact of same, think of this person as dictatorial and oppressive. Under stress, the Emperor does become a tyrant. To exercise control, the Emperor lashes out and seeks to make people and things bend to his or her will. Pushed further, and the Emperor gives up, becoming a grudging slave to situations and people.

Main Summary: Power, leadership, authority, stability, government, order (organized, categorized), rational (realism/objectivity), security, continuity (victory), warm yet committed to the task at hand, courage and determination.

Bottom Line Interpretations (Tarantino): Whatever you have wanted to do—now is the time to do it. If you are willing to jump, you will land on your feet. Negative: get organized. You've been wasting valuable time spinning your wheels. If you put a plan in place before you act, you'll increase your chance for success.

CORRESPONDENCES:

- *Number*: 4, form, manifestation
- *Hebrew*: 5, Tzaddi, צ, fish hook
- *Positive*: Creation, recognition, stability, realism, responsiveness
- *Negative*: Despotism, self-complacency, poorness of feelings, lack of fantasy, rationalism as a prison
- *Zodiac*: Aries (courageous, me first), the Ram, forerunning, always charging ahead
- *Planet*: Mars (aggression, hostility, destruction)
- *Tree of life*: The axis Netzach (Certainty/sensitivity/anarchy)–Yesod (Reflection/imagination)
- *Element*: Fire
- *Life Themes*:

    "I am the sum total of all my authority."
    "And they will know me by my presence."

- *Basic Divinatory Meaning:* (instruction booklet) War, conquest, victory, strife, stability, power, originality, government, energy, ambition. Ill-dignified: overweening pride, megalomania, rashness, ill-temper. (Webster): The card is usually associated with worldly rather than spiritual matters. The person is likely to be taking on more responsibility, or starting a new, ambitious venture. It can sometimes indicate that someone with "Emperor" qualities will help the person get on track.

- *Advice:* Play by the rules and don't take shortcuts. Use common sense when managing your resources. Now is the time to get organized and make plans. Careful use of logic and reason will deliver success. Alternately: Despite your obvious talents, success comes slowly at this time. Respect the past and learn from it. Frustrations, obstacles, delays, or setbacks will test your perseverance. Don't react too hastily; make sure all your decisions are unemotional. Balance work and play.

SYMBOLISM:

- The Emperor is the form and action to the Empress' inspiration and raw potential. This is why the Emperor looks to the right, toward the Empress, from whom he receives his creative ideas;
- He symbolizes the universal principle of personal power and leadership, while also representing the archetype of the pioneer, builder, doer and mystic visionary; serving also as guide, protector and paternal Father. The Emperor's number is four;
- He is akin to the swift, decisive, creative energy of the universe, the initiative of all beings;
- He has an optimistic, warm energetic demeanor while at the same time being totally committed to the task at hand;
- The Emperor holds a ram staff indicating the will to assert his will, where the Empress holds a lotus, signaling willingness for openness and devotion;
- The flow and breath of divine fire sparkles deeply within the aura of the Emperor, bringing structure, order and regulation, which balances the free-flowing, nurturing and lavish abundance of the Empress. His legs are folded in the number 4, an indication of stability, power, and authority;
- He is the traveler who holds the globe of the world, and has the ability to bring solid and secure stability for all, symbolized by the coins on the throne;
- The sun rises behind the throne, bringing nature's beauty and compassion, the glorious rays invigorating the sun of the morning;
- The Maltese cross symbolizes that the channeled energy has reached a successful issue, and the Emperor's individual government has been established;
- Aries the Ram figures prominently within the Emperor's personality; the wayward explorer who with innate curiosity and initiative, journeys into the realms of life for experience and adventure, with the innovative healing passions swirling through the beyond, providing dynamic and initiatory power, the yang, animus, the masculine principle; the ancient and manifested element being Zeus, father of the Gods;
- Tzaddi, also known as the fish hook refers to Aries in the Zodiac, ruled by Mars and hence the sun is exalted. This stream of energy is manifest in

material form, with the idea celebrated in unique and personal authority. The ram by nature, is a wild and courageous animal, stable in lonely places, making the journey exciting and glowing;

- The white light which descends upon the Emperor indicates the position within the sacred Tree of Life. His authority is derived from Chokmah, the Creative Wisdom and Word, and is exerted upon Tiphareth, the organized man;
- The bees on the Emperor's cloak symbolize industriousness and the need for leadership to have vision; seeing and alternating between differing forms of perception. Bumble bees also appear on the Empress and Art/Temperance forms;
- The globe in his hand indicates that he is a builder, activist;
- The fleur-de-lis, the three pronged flame symbolizes the union of mind, heart and spirit, reminding that leadership requires merging within, flowing the peace and sensitivity of negotiation, which is symbolized by the lamb with the flag;
- The lamb indicates his willingness to sacrifice, the flag, an indication that he is willing to "take up the cause;"
- The double phoenix on the shield symbolizes change and transformation, which manifest both internally and externally; the red tincture of the alchemist and the nature of gold, being one with the authority of cosmic harmony;
- The eagle stands on the Emperor's right (in contrast to the Empress) symbolizing the conscious ruling of matter.

INTERPRETATION:

The Emperor is the father figure of the Tarot deck. He is the "provider" and protects and defends his loved ones. He has established a solid family line and is often seen as the patriarch of a wide network of family members. He offers guidance, advice and wisdom to others and in doing so, demonstrates authority and grounding. His wisdom is obtained through worldly, life experience. He has "been there, done that", and has the battle armor to prove it. He takes what he has learned, and passes it on to the next generation, so someday they can be as wise and powerful as he is. He brings security and comfort to those around him.

The Emperor is also representative of structure and stability. He is able to create order out of chaos by carefully categorizing his thoughts and mapping out what needs to be done to solve the problem. He is a systematic and strategic thinker and is highly organized and coordinated in his approach. He sticks to a plan and ensures he sees it out until the end. Thus, this card indicates that you have a strong desire to see your ideas manifested on the physical plane in the form of material gain or accomplishment. An opportunity will arrive that could be the foundation of a very successful future.

The Emperor reflects rules and regulations. He establishes law and order by applying principles or guidelines to a specific situation. He likes to operate within a defined structure with set boundaries. He respects routine and follows a specific regimen or discipline.

Domination of the mind over the heart is sometimes unwanted or best avoided but with the Emperor, it is necessary and even welcomed. If you are facing difficult choices, you must maintain your concentration and focus. Enjoy the assertiveness and confidence that this self-control and focus brings. Push ahead and do what you know is best. Know that if you can master yourself then you should have little problem mastering the world and everything in it.

The Emperor is a powerful leader who demands authority and dominance. He is most comfortable in a leadership role where he can command and direct others. He likes to be in a position of strength, where he can exert control and bring a sense of organization to his activities. He often represents a solid establishment that is built on strong foundations. As a leader, he rules with a firm but fair hand. He will listen to the advice of others but he will always have the final say. He is not afraid of war and/or conflict and he will not hesitate to use his force and power to protect those he cares about. The privileged few whom he favors always repay him with the loyalty and respect he deserves.

The Emperor heralds status, success and recognition. You will have an earnest desire to be recognized as a strong figure of unquestioned achievement and authority. You will want to be known as the dominant force, the leader and the "expert." Focus your attention completely on your goal and be very careful not to reveal any weaknesses or personal doubt.

If you come across the Emperor in your own life, then you will need to be ready to impress! The Emperor administers and governs the area you wish to enter. You cannot achieve your dreams and goals without this person's blessing. With the Emperor's support, you will have a much better chance of actualizing your dream and you can begin to benefit from the established structure he has formed.

Sometimes, the Emperor can represent the power of the government or a decision-making body. Within yourself, there is also a force that governs your actions. These forces are will power and self-control. You may have discussions concerning contractual agreements, profit sharing, subsidies or management.

DIVINATION:

You may now be asked to take on a position of leadership or authority over a project or others. The Emperor asks you to accept this responsibility and carry out your task with energy and confidence, while also taking care that the power doesn't go to your head (an all too familiar story as history shows)! The ideal is to lead by example through love and service to the people in your care, so that they follow you willingly and joyfully knowing that you have their best interests at heart. Otherwise, you may resort to a bullying dictatorship where people are forced to obey your tyrannical demands through fear.

This is a propitious moment for a change or a new beginning. Trust your own energy and move with it.

If you have been subject to a series of seemingly natural (unsuspected) catastrophes or disruptions, it may indicate the failure to identify and address unconscious factors and emotions not best addressed in a linear, conscious fashion.

Questions to ponder: What revitalization does your life need? What have you wanted to do for some time now? Are there steps you would like to take toward this? Are you willing to take a step now?

Affirmation to give yourself: I trust my power. I rule by serving. I serve by ruling.

V. THE HEIROPHANT

TAROTNYMS

Strength by loyalty, conviction versus dull/uncreative/going too slow

Knowledge/Wisdom versus lack of flexibility/dogmatic

Open/searching for truth versus gullible/ignoring practical matters/longing for more meaning

The importance of convention/structure/routine versus the need for something new/results

SOMEONE ELSE'S (TRADITION/MENTOR) PATH

SNAPSHOT

WISDOM/ADVISOR (TEACHER)/DOCTRINE (CONVICTION)/TRADITION (LOYALTY)

BAUTA "HIDING PLACE" QUADRANT (SCOTT GROSSBERG):^

The Mask: Search for Truth	The Beast: Rigid
What makes me who I am; How I view myself; What I'm attracted to; What I take for granted in myself.	How others view me; What I excuse in myself; My deepest urge; What I resort to under stress.
The Shadow: Enabling	The Light: Tolerant
The thing I have no wish to be; What I think I've left behind; What I become when all else fails; What I still must learn to control.	What others think I need; What I look at with wonder; What I need for balance; What I desire to accomplish.

MEANING:

The Hierophant finds it much easier to go along with convention and to conform to the accepted modes of the era. While simply trying to help make sense of the world, others view him/her as quite strict and unbending. The Hierophant becomes unbending and intolerant when under stress, as if the numerous rules and regulations s/he values are a sacred talisman against obstacles. When pushed into a corner, the Hierophant quickly becomes accommodating, letting rules fall by the wayside. In order to achieve more balance, the Hierophant needs to exercise more tolerance and permissiveness rather than advocating and administering harsh decrees.

Main Summary: Spiritual, search for hidden truths, discovery of meaning, knowledge, conforming, intolerance, esoteric nonsense.

Bottom Line Interpretations (Tarantino): Now is not a good time for innovative strategies. Stick to a more conservative approach and go with what you know works. Negative: Time to re-evaluate your plan. You are drowning in "should's" and "ought to's." Rely on your own experiences. Trust yourself; do what you want and need to, not what you think you should do.

CORRESPONDENCES:

- *Number*: 5, as quintessence, the power that exceeds the four elements, union of spirit and earth
- *Hebrew*: 6, Vau, ו, Nail
- *Positive*: Search for knowledge and illumination, the desire to study creed and dogma instead of simply accepting them, to research and achieve further development. It also stands for the deep fulfillment someone can find when really trusting their own beliefs.
- *Negative*: bigotry, the blind faith in dogma, intolerance towards everything different from one's own confession. It can also mean gullibility, running to any kind of new belief just because the traditional one is suddenly considered boring or unsatisfying.
- *Zodiac*: Taurus (strength)
- *Planet*: Venus (beauty)
- *Tree of Life*: From Chokmah (Energy/wisdom) to Chesed, (Power/stability)
- Element: Earth
- *Life Themes*:

    "I am the sum of all my fears."
    "And they will know me by my concessions."

- *Basic Divinatory Meaning*: (instruction booklet) Divine wisdom, inspiration, stubborn, strength, toil, endurance, persistence, teaching, help from superiors, patience, organization, peace, goodness of heart, occult force voluntary invoked. (Webster): Represents a spiritual person who is also a teacher and advisor. The person is looking for answers to deep spiritual or philosophical questions.
- *Advice:* Follow the path that is familiar. Now is a good time to show how conventional you can be. Your public image and status with friends or in the community are of great concern to you now. Don't sacrifice your beliefs

or freedoms for status. Keep alert to the outside world. Alternately: Make things happen by taking care of details. Don't become too rigidly attached to order and routine—the ritual shouldn't mean more to you than the result. Personal growth comes through modesty and compassion.

SYMBOLISM:

- Many of the symbols on the card refer to these ideas of structure, authority and spirituality;
- The four "masks" in the corners are the symbols of the four powers of the sphinx (to know, to will, to dare, to keep silent);
- The large bull is the symbol of Taurus (which this card is assigned to) giving strength, earthiness, tenacity, loyalty, commitment, and stability;
- The elephants are also for strength, solidity and memory of the past;
- The face of the Hierophant looks somewhat like a mask, suggesting a lack of flexibility or perhaps an outward role that hides and inner truth;
- The wand with three rings symbolize, the Aeons of Isis, Osiris, and Horus (union of body, mind, and soul);
- The open hand points to the earth indicating willingness to share knowledge.

INTERPRETATION:

The Hierophant represents our innate need to make sense of our experiences by aligning them with a higher, unified purpose.

He is a symbol for a world of belief and confession, may it be a church, a sect or an occult society. He's the pope (a word which means, "bridge"), the druid or the High Priest in a system of creeds and dogmas. He represents the religious and intellectual tradition of a person, and may be the one the person is born to it or possibly the one who has chosen it by himself.

The Hierophant symbolizes the principle of learning and teaching, emanating the trust in faith and inspirational ideas, shining with divine wisdom, having stubborn strength, persistence and endurance. The concept of family is represented, teaching that when goodness shines within, anything is possible. As you teach, so you will learn and that what you teach is instructing your spirit.

The Hierophant often refers to trust, search for truth, experience of meaning, power of conviction, virtue, expansion of consciousness, and strength of faith. It also cautions against arrogant self-complacency and a dogmatic know-it-all attitude.

DIVINATION:

As a card for the day it speaks of it being a day to defer to authority, or to consult with a mentor. Generally it would suggest it's a good time to learn from a person already in possession of knowledge, particularly if they are part of an institution. It might also suggest today is a good day to look a little deeper, to understand the deeper, more spiritual, meanings of the life going on around you.

Involve yourself with the teachings of spiritual masters. Seek the presence of a master or teacher. Involve yourself in groups for personal growth. Be honest, open and receptive in these groups. Pay attention to the instructions of your heart.

Questions to ponder: To facilitate this situation, what do I need to learn? Is there any master of wisdom (past or present) to whom you feel attracted? What values and beliefs have I been taught that no longer apply?

Affirmation to give yourself: There is only one voice worth listening to, the voice of my own heart.

VI. THE LOVERS

TAROTNYMS

In balance, harmony, unity versus loss/giving up of one's self/unable to bring opposites together

Sense of meaning/oneness with self and world versus searching but yet to find purpose/beliefs/feeling of shallowness

Knowing one's chosen path/deepest, secret wishes/desires but unable/frightened (and for good, common sense reasons)

An important choice has been made or is on the threshold versus can't decide which way to go/doesn't want to or know what to let go of

FINDING YOUR PATH

SNAPSHOT

UNITY/THINGS COMING TOGETHER/HARMONY/ATTRACTON/UNDERSTANDING/WHOLENESS

BAUTA "HIDING PLACE" QUADRANT (SCOTT GROSSBERG):

The Mask: Connected/Attracted	The Beast: Obsessive
What makes me who I am; How I view myself; What I'm attracted to; What I take for granted in myself.	How others view me; What I excuse in myself; My deepest urge; What I resort to under stress.
The Shadow: Detached	The Light: Unconcerned
The thing I have no wish to be; What I think I've left behind; What I become when all else fails; What I still must learn to control.	What others think I need; What I look at with wonder; What I need for balance; What I desire to accomplish.

MEANING:

Great responsibility is felt. Wants to please those with whom they are intimate. When stressed, s/he becomes obsessive. Pushed to the limits, the person becomes detached, acting "as if" s/he is uninterested, even uncaring, although the desire for union remains. To achieve balance, the person must address and overcome fear of loss and abandonment, engaging with others with an untroubled air.

Main Summary: Choice, intellect, attraction (especially to ideas), inspiration, harmonizing of opposites, aesthetics.

Bottom Line Interpretations (Tarantino): It is through our interaction with the world and others that we discover who we are and come to understand how we fit in the world. New or deepening relationship, project or situation. An opportunity to come to know yourself better. Negative: You are repressing your own needs and needs while engaging in this relationship project, or situation. If unwilling to change the structure of your relationship or work, it will become brittle and break.

CORRESPONDENCES:

- *Number*: 6, combination of contrast and their mutual penetration, harmony and equilibrium restored
- *Hebrew*: 7, Zain, ז, Sword
- *Positive*: Full-hearted confession, trust, optimism
- *Negative*: Displacement, repression, giving up on one's self
- *Zodiac*: Gemini (sign of duality), giving the ability to attract opposites
- *Planet*: Mercury (will and swiftness), giving strong mental capacity
- *Tree of life*: 17, From Binah (understanding) to Tiphareth, (balance)
- *Element*: Air
- *Life Themes*:

    "I am the sum total of those who love me."
    "And they will know me by my loyalty."

- *Basic Divinatory Meaning*: (instruction booklet) Openness to inspiration, intuition, intelligence, childishness, attraction, beauty, love. Ill-dignified: self-contradiction, instability, indecision. Union in a shallow degree with others. Superficial. (Webster): A card of "choice." The person may need to make a difficult decision between two opposing possibilities. Often this choice is between heart and head.
- *Advice*: Lovers and close friends take center stage. Take the time to tell those closest to you what they mean to you. Examine all of your relationships that are going nowhere—eliminate the unwanted and unnecessary. Alternately: exaggeration abounds, emotions run high--especially jealousy. Beware of self-indulgence and greed. Slow down. Don't let anyone rush you or push you into things.

SYMBOLISM:

- The orphic egg with snake, symbols of transformation through relationship;
- The images of Lilith and Eve (primal feminine energy) in the upper corners of the Lovers card and Cain and Abel (masculine energy) as the children;

- The latter together hold the Holy Grail and sword, indicative of the quest through mind and intuition;
- One holds a club (penis, masculine energy); the other, flowers (creativity).

Here we have the two who will to become the one. The black king with his golden crown and sacred lance, wearing the serpent-adorned robe of the Emperor, the alchemical sulphur or energizing force, and the White Queen with her silver crown and her Holy Grail (a golden cup engraved with the descending dove of Holy Spirit), wearing the bees of the Empress, the alchemical salt awaiting energizing:

- They are here to take part in the hermetic marriage, their willingness conveyed by their joined hands. Standing beneath an arch of swords, not only symbolizing the Hebrew correspondence, but also being the weapon of nobility, it honors their marriage and acknowledges their sovereignty. It is not just a love, but love under will. All dualities are here represented by the royal pair, ready to be united or melded into one;
- Cupid symbolizes attraction.

The Hermit performs the ceremony, a symbol of hidden knowledge:

- He is the largest figure in the image;
- The scroll wrapped around his arms, indicates the wisdom he possesses;
- The pink robe indicates his unconditional love and understanding.

INTERPRETATION:

The card also represents a decision, the farewell to a former way of life and the full acceptance of love uncompromising. It doesn't necessarily mean that the 'love' is a person—it can be a passion, a desire, or even a profession. Many people who lead an adapted, settled life actually have deep desires and hidden wishes, that they don't dare show, which they constantly fight, suppressing their own happiness.

The Lovers can mean that someone should be honest, make a clear decision for this love, the fulfilling of a wish, of a desire, and stand by it.

The Lovers can say that a peaceful combination of existing contrasts or contradictions is a better solution than any confrontation—diplomacy instead of war.

Many books define the card not as "Love" but as a "choice." And the fruit from the Tree of Knowledge indicates Adam and Eve choosing to "know" each other in every sense of the word.

The connection to Gemini means that the Lovers card is NOT about "romance" or passion. Romantic emotions are typically related to water. And blazing passion is associated with fire. Gemini, an air sign, is about messages and making contact. It's about the psyche.

In addition, the number 6 the Lover's card is about "harmony."

In a reading it will always indicate a "choice." The petitioner knows what they want, but they don't want to give anything up. This card indicates that the choice is going to bring a "good-bye" to someone, or something. The surrounding cards will reveal the nature of the "choice," and sometimes even the outcome.

To be complete, we need to integrate the dualities within.

DIVINATION:

The card indicates that the petitioner has come across, or will come across a person, career, challenge or thing (a puppy, a car, a house) that they will fall in love with. They will know instinctively that it was meant for them, even if it means diverging from their chosen path (that is the "Love" part). On the other hand, their common sense must also make a decision on whether or not to go along with this psychic "choice." There is often a measure of hardship or cost that comes with giving into this spiritual attraction.

Two choices are involved with the card. First, your soul or psyche is making its choice. It recognizes this other person/thing as being your spiritual twin or as harmonizing with you; you become "amorous" for it.

Now the rest of you, the demands of your life, your emotional heart, passionate soul, can agree or not. That's the other choice. You will feel powerfully drawn to this career, challenge, person or thing so much so that, no matter how scary, how difficult, irrational or troublesome, you will be inclined to go for it. This is LOVE. But you will also know that it comes at a cost.

Questions to ponder: What do you seek in the people you love? What comprises a fulfilling relationship for you? Am I willing/capable of taking responsibility for my own needs? What adjustments do I need to make to move forward with this relationship?

Affirmation to give yourself: I am now ready to meet the partner I've always longed to meet.

VII. THE CHARIOT

TAROTNYMS

Significant forward movement and direction/moving forward/action taken/triumph over difficulties versus held back/encountering barriers/running over (insensitivity) to others

Marshalling energies from within versus a need to protect one's self from hostile forces while pursuing one's own desires

Packed up/ready to go versus lack of opportunities/no practical plan/destination

ON YOUR PATH

SNAPSHOT

MOMENTUM/TRIUMPH/MOTION/STRENGTH/STABILITY

BAUTA "HIDING PLACE" QUADRANT (SCOTT GROSSBERG):

The Mask: Strength What makes me who I am; How I view myself; What I'm attracted to; What I take for granted in myself.	The Beast: Fearless How others view me; What I excuse in myself; My deepest urge; What I resort to under stress.
The Shadow: Cowardly The thing I have no wish to be; What I think I've left behind; What I become when all else fails; What I still must learn to control.	The Light: Timid What others think I need; What I look at with wonder; What I need for balance; What I desire to accomplish.

MEANING:

Success after overcoming obstacles. A conqueror who feels victorious. It is important that others see this person as dauntless and courageous. Others remember this person's bravado. When encountering opposition (stress), more swagger is displayed. Pushed to extremes, can take the opposite approach, becoming cowardly, fearful, and distrusting of his/her own talents. To achieve balance, must stop or decrease the outward displays and adopt a more measured, cautious, reflective stance.

Main Summary: Strong-willed, strength, triumph. Protected, shielded, defended, victory, and health. Success, though sometimes not stable and enduring. Travel.

Bottom Line Interpretations (Tarantino): The struggle is over and a new adventure is about to begin. Perfect time to initiate any major lifestyle change. Hard work has guaranteed a successful outcome. Negative: The situation is unpredictable and could easily get out of control. Hiding your needs only contributes to your feeling like a victim. Be guided solely by whether or not your decisions/behavior leads to your goal.

CORRESPONDENCES:

- *Number*: 7, as the number of earthly and divine harmony (3+4), destiny, motion, expansion
- *Hebrew*: 8, Chet, ח, Fence
- *Positive*: The awakening of powers, the way ahead, searching and finding one's place in life
- *Negative*: Megalomania, insensitivity, running against walls
- *Zodiac*: Cancer (receptivity)
- *Planet*: Moon (inner, imagination, unconscious, reflective, illusive, emotion)/Jupiter (luck and expansion)
- *Tree of life*: 18, the way from Binah (understanding) to Geburah, (movement)
- *Element*: Water
- *Life Themes*:

   "I am the sum of all my rage."
   "And they shall know me by my self-restraint."

- *Basic Divinatory Meaning*: (instruction booklet) Triumph, victory, hope, obedience, faithfulness, health, success, though sometimes not enduring. Authority under authority. Ill-dignified: violence in maintaining traditional ideas. Lust of destruction. (Webster): Change, travel, triumph over difficulties, obstacles, and competition from others.
- *Advice*: Victories are on your horizon. Reject negative people but don't judge them harshly. Appeal to others' sense of fair play. This is a very good time for travel, taking a break, and getting away. Alternately: People are more defensive now. Don't give in to intimidation or pressure. No one wants to waste time. Expect last minute cancellation of plans.

SYMBOLISM:

- An armored knight, on a hero's journey (ready to do battle) with the crab of the zodiac sign Cancer mounted on his head, a symbol of the tendency to zig zag when he travels;

- He is sitting Indian-style, wearing a red cape, while bearing the Holy Grail, a symbol that he holds the potential in his hands. He does not hold the handles (like a shield); instead he cradles the logos in comfort;
- The center of the Grail is blood-red and in the shape of the full moon, representing energy and connection to the unconscious;
- Jupiterian waves emanate outwards, but the charioteer's shield encloses them into his apparatus;
- The rider has no means of control, indicating that we must confront whatever divine (life) forces takes us, trusting our four basic faculties;
- The red cape indicates the bloodshed while protecting the Grail early on his path, and shows that he has learned from those experiences;
- His amber colored armor has the "Ten Stars of Assaiah" on the chest and shoulders, which would indicate an inheritance of occult talent and skills;
- The visor is closed and the armor protects every inch of the knight. Crowley wrote in the Book of Thoth, "For no man may look upon the face and live;"
- The Chariot is a symbol of moving out into the world:
- The four pillars are made from the wood of Baphomet's tree and represent the "Four Pillars of the Universe," indicating the aspirant's current developmental level, and even his place in the ongoing initiation process;
- The red wheels indicate the revolving motions influenced by Geburah, and the blue canopy reflects the night sky of Binah;
- The canopy is emblazed with the word abraHADabra, indicating that the aspirant has successfully transmuted the destructive Martian energies into the physical assistance and spiritual contentment of the very experienced Knight;
- The chariot is pulled by the four sphinxes who are also cherubs, symbolizing thinking, feeling, sensing, intuiting. The bull, the lion, the eagle, and the man are the sphinxes, but looking closely; all four cherub's bodies have been counter-switched which would indicate the sixteen sub-elements. This is the result of theurgy, and the mastering of the elemental realms, even an ultra-balanced elemental kingdom, hinting at the secret apparatus of "Equilibrium." Note that the rider sits above these faculties, exalting his mental/reflective capabilities while still staying in touch with all;

- Behind the chariot is the influence of the Supernals descending through the veil, which would be an aspect of Sepirothic path 18 between the divine power of Binah and the whirling motions of Geburah;
- While the supernals push, the Sphinxes pull the Chariot down a yellow brick road, the latter a symbol of developing his own identity;
- The hieroglyph as a whole indicates protection at its fullest, and finest. This luxury is not without cost. It has been a long tough road, and your decisions have been of sound moral character, the reward is the protected state of the VII Chariot, and the working formulae of the Holy Grail.

INTERPRETATION:

The Chariot stands for combined powers, ready to move forward. It represents the dynamic principle and the human will to proceed, the ability to use the powers of life and keep the outer and inner balance.

The Chariot shows a strong will, a strong personality, and at its best, victory and success. But it also is a symbol for controversial power, for contradictions that are not solved, but just controlled. In this, the trump also warns of overestimation and recklessness. With every new venture or beginning one should check carefully whether the desired goal is compatible with one's life and inner self.

Additionally, the Chariot is a symbol for the armor we build up when moving forward in the process of self-assertion. It also alludes to the danger that we might mix this armor with our actual personality.

So a negative aspect of the Chariot might involve understanding that the way of armed power isn't always the right one that the controversial power inside may to be reconciled with one other, and not just controlled and suppressed.

In spiritual matters: Light in the Darkness. The burden you carry may be the Holy Grail.

In matters of the heart: Faithfulness. Hope. Obedience. A protective relationship.

In intellectual matters: Firm, even violent adherence to dogma or tradition.

In material matters: Victory. Triumph. Chain of command.

DIVINATION:

Most petitioners want to know about the future; they want to know if they are going to be safe and secure. The Chariot indicates that the petitioner is fully protected. This card usually comes up when the petitioner is sure of impending disaster; so when you smile and tell them that "everything is perfect", and that "they are protected" on the path of whatever the overall reading is indicating.

The oncoming change promises to lead to a positive phase in your life. Ready yourself, put your affairs in order, and examine the possibilities. You will leave much behind.

Questions to ponder: What area of your life will be changing? Are you ready to ring out the old and ring in the new? Is this action moving you closer or further away from your goals?

Affirmation to give yourself: I am putting my life in order and preparing for the new beginning.

VIII. ADJUSTMENT:

TAROTNYMS

An equilibrium in matters and life, keeping balls in the air versus life being out of balance, just beyond one's sense of control

Recognizing and adjusting to the realities of life versus pushing forward with one's own agenda despite consequence

Fairness/ability to look at both sides versus feeling life has not been fair/tendency to be self-righteous

See the truth/cut through the nonsense versus insensitive/interpersonally costly

ABLE TO ADJUST/ACCEPT PAST INJUSTICES AND MOVE ON/CONTENT VERSUS NURSING OLD GRUDGES/HURTS THAT KEEP THE PERSON FROM MOVING ON OR CONSTANT ACCEPTANCE THAT CAUSES A LOSS OF SELF

SNAPSHOTS

CONFRONTING REALITY
RECOVERY/RESTORATION/BALANCE/SETTING THE SCALES STRAIGHT

BAUTA "HIDING PLACE" QUADRANT (SCOTT GROSSBERG):

The Mask: Balance What makes me who I am; How I view myself; What I'm attracted to; What I take for granted in myself.	The Beast: Dispassionate How others view me; What I excuse in myself; My deepest urge; What I resort to under stress.
The Shadow: Unfair The thing I have no wish to be; What I think I've left behind; What I become when all else fails; What I still must learn to control.	The Light: Passionate What others think I need; What I look at with wonder; What I need for balance; What I desire to accomplish.

MEANINGS:

A strong value of balance, karma, discipline, and teamwork. To others, may be seen as unemotional and uncaring, when in fact the person is a realist. Under stress, the person may switch off emotions and rely on cold, hard facts. Although disliking inequity and injustice, when pushed, this person reveals those very traits, becoming unjust, biased, and one not above hitting "below the belt." To maintain balance, the person needs to spend more time with people and circumstances that arouse hopes, dreams, and passions.

Main Summary: Balance of contrasts, justice, homeostasis, karma, fairness, uncompromising honesty and objectivity, the realization of cause and effect, background and consequence, not deceived by appearances.

Bottom Line Interpretations (Tarantino): Postpone plans until the pros and cons have been carefully considered. Look at the situation from all angles. Be sure you are on firm ground. The more you know, the better. Remain flexible and willing to change course. Check out the legalities. Negative: You may be caught temporarily in an unjust situation. May feel like you are caught in a juggling act where any moves causes a loss of equilibrium. Nothing can be done in the short run. In the long run, justice will prevail.

CORRESPONDENCES:

- *Number*: 8, as the number of justice, adjustment (2 x 4, 2 x 2 etc.), stability through change
- *Hebrew*: 30, ל, Lamed, Ox goad
- *Positive*: Balance, justice, fairness, always looking at both sides
- *Negative*: Self-righteousness
- *Zodiac*: Libra (balance)
- *Planet*: Venus (beauty)
- *Tree of life*: The connection between Geburah (understanding) and Tiphareth (balance).
- *Element*: Air
- *Life Themes*:

   "I am the sum of all my innocence."
   "And they will know me by my mercy."

- *Basic Divinatory Meaning*: (instruction booklet) Justice, balance, adjustment, equilibrium, suspension of action, pending decision, karma, the card of systemic thinking. May refer to lawsuits, trials, marriages, treatises, etc. (Webster): Right will prevail. Choice that must be examined carefully before a decision is made. The person must act in an honest, fair, upright manner to insure success.
- *Advice*: What goes around comes around. Seek legal counsel, ask advice from elders. You may be embroiled in negotiations or tedious bureaucratic systems. Do healthy things—spiritually and physically. Alternately: Tell the truth or get ready to suffer the consequences. Your friends are wishy-washy now. Do your part to say what's real, what's right, and what you feel. Let go of the past and resolve to turn over a new leaf.

SYMBOLISM:

The female figure holds "the bubbles of Maya," typifying the transitory quality of human justice." As far as the life-path was concerned, this could mean a realization in the individual of the unfairness of life, and the need to "adjust accordingly" and think out personal methods of settling conflicts in as just and fair a way as possible:

- She is standing on her tiptoes, the balls of her feet placed against the blade of the sword that she has in her hands, indicating alertness to the compensation that needs to be made from moment to moment;
- On her forehead is the Uraeus serpent which is Lord of Life and Death (Alpha and Omega);
- The feathered cape (made of ostrich plumes) of Maat, the Egyptian goddess of justice who weighed the souls of the newly departed against a feather to determine the balance between their humanness and divinity;
- Her face is masked but not enough to hide her expression of secret satisfaction in her dominion over all the de-stabilizing elements in the Universe. It indicates a lack of preconceptions, and ability to rely on her inner wisdom to keep a sense of balance;
- Her crown is formed as if it is a testes and lingua shape head piece;
- The scales hang from the crown with a delicate balance, the pans weighing the first sphere alpha equally and exactly against the last, omega;
- The first and last spheres show up in the hand guard on the hilt of the magic sword of the Magus, held between her thighs, representing logic;
- The cross made by her body represent a balance of the four elements;
- The throne of pyramids and spheres (4 in number signifying Law and Limitation), on which she is poised, represents the same equity that she herself manifests. Outside the throne are balanced light and dark spheres, both equal and opposite indicating that the universe is not necessarily just/fair, but it is exact;
- Four globes, one at each corner of the card, and lines seem to radiate everywhere: from her shoulders, her legs, and from the four globes in harlequin-like patterns. The card vibrates with an energy of power and authority that is yet rendered stable if animated;

- The card is full of blue and yellow, and greens that come from the combination of these two colors. It is all about symmetry.

INTERPRETATION:

In nature, there is no justice, merely the co-existence of all.

The card uses the image of Libra (logically, the astrological sign associated with this card). By doing so, we move beyond human laws and enter the sphere of universal law. Going back to the notion of energy, Adjustment concerns itself with a more detached form of judgment: that of the desire of the universe always to find balance, to find its energetic integrity. It may fall in line with our moral laws but it is ultimately disinterested in them.

The Adjustment card is seen in the "Butterfly effect," as all equilibrium must and will be obtained. Any disturbance will be balanced by an equal and opposite reaction. What you put out, you will get back. Think well, think love, and all will be well in thought and deed.

DIVINATION:

The person is or soon will be faced with a choice that should be carefully considered before making a decision. Act in an open, upright, honest fashion in order to succeed.

Whatever you decide to do on your daily travels, it is totally up to you. Whether good, bad or indifferent, nature will redeem herself, and she will do this with a smile. She will do this with the sword. The sword teaches. Nature is not always fair, but she is just.

This card could sometimes hint at friends that are not really your friends. Or those times when you remember and review situations that seem regretful. These things are not fun but they are a part of life. These painful situations and their introspection usually result in growth.

Pay attention to what situations in your daily life tend to throw you off-balance. Discover the conditions under which you find harmony again. Carry this quality with you as you move through your daily activities.

Questions to ponder: What helps you to reach your meditative center, and to stay there? What happens when you lose your center? Am I willing to stay open to new possibilities, avoid rushing to premature conclusions? Do I have all the information I need? How can I remain flexible and willing to re-evaluate the situation, consider alternative ways to obtain the results?

Affirmation to give yourself: I am at rest in my own center.

IX. THE HERMIT:

TAROTNYMS

Looking ardently for one's own path/searching within/trusting self versus isolated/disconnected/lonely/fear of others and life

Inner wisdom versus arrogant/cold

On a personal quest/journey versus neglecting day to day, practical matters/relationships

REFLECTING ON YOUR PATH IN LIGHT OF EXPERIENCE

SNAPSHOTS

INTROSPECTION/REFLECTION/INNER LIFE/INSIGHT/WISDOM

BAUTA "HIDING PLACE" QUADRANT (SCOTT GROSSBERG):

The Mask: Searcher/Introspective What makes me who I am; How I view myself; What I'm attracted to; What I take for granted in myself.	**The Beast:** Unsociable How others view me; What I excuse in myself; My deepest urge; What I resort to under stress.
The Shadow: Familiar The thing I have no wish to be; What I think I've left behind; What I become when all else fails; What I still must learn to control.	**The Light:** Friendly What others think I need; What I look at with wonder; What I need for balance; What I desire to accomplish.

MEANINGS:

On a search for knowledge. The person values solitude, maybe a loner at heart, although does not feel alone when by him/herself. Others view this person as unsociable. When stressed becomes unfriendly and anti-social. When unable to escape, s/he takes the opposite course, seeming to become intimate with everyone around. To all appearances, everyone is a friend. To maintain balance, this person needs to be less self-absorbed and more amiable with those who live around him/her.

Main Summary: Contemplation, completion, introspection, humility, not ruled by materialism.

Bottom Line Interpretations (Tarantino): Time for solitude and reflection to sort through the information you've gathered, determine where you are at this point, and what is important to you. The light cast by your vision is the only one needed to illuminate your path. Negative: time to confront the past and resolve any conflicting issues. Seclusion, which began as healing, only contributes to loneliness and isolation. Time to move back into the world.

CORRESPONDENCES:

- *Number*: 9, ending of a cycle, completion, as the number going back into itself (3 x 3)
- *Hebrew*: 10, Yod, י, Hand
- *Positive*: Wisdom, realization, mental maturity, the inner light, introspection/reflection (thinking things over, changes, endings of cycles, focusing inward, concentrating less on external senses, quieting yourself, looking for answers within, needing to understand), seeker of truth (seeking greater understanding, looking for something, wanting truth at all costs, going on a personal quest, discoveries and revelations, questions and problem-solving, psychological analysis of self), seeking solitude (needing to be alone, desiring stillness, withdrawing from the world, experiencing seclusion, giving up distractions, retreating into a private world, silence and patience), receiving and giving guidance (going to/being a mentor, accepting/offering wise council, learning from/being a sage turning to/being a trusted guide, being helped/helping others, heightened perception and inspiration, rest and relaxation).
- *Negative*: Numbness, loneliness, bitterness, unhealthy reclusiveness, aloofness and loneliness, elitism and intellectual arrogance, abstraction, narcissism, conservatism and prejudice, inhibition, criticalness, cunning and manipulation, fussiness and nitpicking, bickering and undue hesitation, suspicion and coldness, hate, infirmity and death.
- *Zodiac*: Virgo, symbolized by the fertile wheat is mutable Earth and attends to details, organization and beauty
- *Planet*: Mercury (will and swiftness)
- *Tree of life*: From Chesed (Power of growth/stability/condensation) to Tiphareth (Balance/middle/harmony)
- *Element*: Earth
- *Life Themes*:

    "I am the sum of all my sadness."
    "And they shall know me by my solitude."

- *Basic Divinatory Meaning*: (instruction booklet) Illumination from within. Divine inspiration. Wisdom. Prudence. Circumspection. Retirement from participation in current events. (Webster): The person needs time on his or her own to contemplate, meditate, reflect, study, and pause. He or she needs "time out" to think something through.

- *Advice*: Break an unnecessary habit. Take steps to eliminate unhealthy ruts and routines. Have some of your friends been driving you crazy? Now is a good time to get them out of your life. Don't let yourself get stuck in the expectations of others. Alternately: spend time with someone you love; take care of unfinished business. Don't let your responsibilities weigh you down and stay away from anything that goes against your grain.

SYMBOLISM:

- Yod, the letter, means hand. The Hermit resembles the shape of the Hebrew character which is the foundation of all characters. Hand = self. All starts with the individual. The power is in their hand;

- The Hermit, a figure representing solitude and introversion, wears the blood-red cloak, Binah, the Egyptian symbol of gestation, representing integrity and honesty within oneself. Green, yellow, slate-grey, green-grey and plum are also colors associated with the wise guide and sage;

- Nurture and touch are important facets of the Hermit; the solar light is held by the hand, which, as noted above, is the Hebrew letter Yod, the 10th letter;

- He is turned away indicating that he has turned his back on the external world;

- The fertile field of wheat is a representation of the fertility of his mind, the spermatozoa, creativity, and procreation;

- The poisonous snake represents (along with Cerberus) the danger filled realms of exploring one's own shadow;

- Cerberus, the three-headed watchdog is the guardian of the underworld and symbolizes the facet of completion; one head is looking to the past and two to the present moment and the future. This ideology is symbolic of the shadow self, which must be explored and incorporated before wholeness of self can be achieved;

- In amongst the wheat of fertility is found the orphic egg; the serpent wrapped around the egg, the symbol of giving birth to new and abundant spiritual forms which manifest into the material plane of life and Spirit;
- The color red represents honesty, integrity; green, creativity and regeneration; white, purity, clarity; gold, malleability.

INTERPRETATION:

The Hermit represents retirement from the outside world, introversion into the inner self, listening to the inner voice and caring for the inner self. He requires retreat from any 'high life' and loud company, and stands for a time of self-reflection and self-realization.

For most people, the silent loneliness of the Hermit appears unattractive, but behind the Hermit is the wisdom of the High Priestess. You cannot listen to your inner voices while having a party.

In its negative aspect, the Hermit could mean being afraid of others or of life. When the retreat turns out to be a runaway, the loneliness can turn into a jail.

Bear in mind that once you swing the light of illumination one way, shadow will also come into being. This is a critical aspect of the Hermit, as the journey into the inner core sanctum passes through the realm of shade, where a healthy relationship with your darker aspect is of great benefit.

DIVINATION:

When you have the Hermit as a growth symbol, it is a strong signal to take the time to complete unfinished business from the past and start on a journey of introspection and reflection.

The Hermit signifies a time for retreat, silence and contemplation, where organization and attending to details is the order of the moment. It is a time to release that which is outgrown and no longer usable.

It is a wonderful time to resolve issues and start new adventures with Virgo people. When the sun enters the House of Virgo, you will be completing and initiating new and exciting projects and relationships. New opportunities from older people will also present themselves.

It is a great time to express yourself with your hands through creativity and healing; you will be a lantern guide and sage for yourself and others.

Do not expect to be revered by others, or understood as you go inward. Instead, gather together people who will be supportive on the shared path of finding your inner voice and listening to it.

Questions to ponder: Have you any unresolved situations or relationships in your life? What do I need to let go of to be completely focused on the present moment?

Affirmation to give yourself: I enjoy my aloneness. I can stop being alone whenever I want.

X. FORTUNE:

TAROTNYMS

Be rid of past misfortune/change of fortune/turning around after a difficulty versus being unable to see or flexible enough to seize the opportunity/cynicism/fatalism (nothing can be done)

However prepared, fortune plays a role in the outcome versus I am in complete control

Opportunity favors the prepared mind versus maintaining hope when reality needs to be faced/taking steps to make one's luck

Reaching a crossroads versus lacking the will to make a choice

A new opportunity presents versus the need for stability and security

THE ROLE LUCK/FATE PLAY

SNAPSHOT

LUCK/FATE/CHANCE/CHANGE IS CONSTANT

BAUTA "HIDING PLACE" QUADRANT (SCOTT GROSSBERG):

The Mask: Chance/Destiny What makes me who I am; How I view myself; What I'm attracted to; What I take for granted in myself.	The Beast: Fatalism How others view me; What I excuse in myself; My deepest urge; What I resort to under stress.
The Shadow: Rebellious The thing I have no wish to be; What I think I've left behind; What I become when all else fails; What I still must learn to control.	The Light: Autonomous What others think I need; What I look at with wonder; What I need for balance; What I desire to accomplish.

MEANING:

A sense that what happens is a result of fate, resulting in feelings of helplessness or lack of control, powerlessness, of being subject to (or more positively stated) aware of bigger forces (someone or something). Under stress, the person may fall prey to a deeply held belief that the future is fixed and unchangeable. When pushed beyond resignation, s/he rebels, acting as if Fate be damned, s/he will forge his/her own path. To achieve balance, the person needs to be less focused on destiny and concentrate on making and forging a life s/he desires.

Main Summary: Represents the element of luck. The incalculable factor. Fate. Rotation.

Bottom Line Interpretations (Tarantino): You've reached a major turning point in your life. A period of good fortune follows. Time for contemplation has passed. What is being called for is your immediate, active participation in the project. Be open to the possibilities. Negative: life is continuously evolving. It is inevitable that the present circumstances will change. Opportunity is knocking but you're not opening the door. It may not knock twice.

CORRESPONDENCES:

- *Number*: 10, as symbol for perfection, culmination, new beginning, the cross sum is 1 (the Magician)
- *Hebrew*: 20, Koph, ⬚, closed/open hand
- *Positive*: Unexpected changings, fortune, realization of luck
- *Negative*: Fatalism, a changing for the worse
- *Zodiac*: Sagittarius, the archer (subtle energy, swift, elusive) and Pieces (transition)
- *Planet*: Jupiter (luck, expansion, abundance, wisdom)
- *Tree of life*: Path 21, the axis Chesed (Power of growth/stability/condensation) – Netzach (Creativity/sensitivity/anarchy)
- *Element*: Fire
- *Life Theme*:

   I am the sum of all things that touch me."
   "And they will know me by chance."

- *Basic Divinatory Meaning*: (instruction booklet) change of fortune, generally good. Destiny. Encouraging us to take changes we would not ordinarily take.
- *Advice*: You've made your bed, now you must lie in it. Own up to your actions and responsibilities—or suffer the consequences. Be true to yourself. Try something new. Luck may not be on your side at the moment. May not be a good time to get embroiled in anything you'll regret. This is not a good time to be alone. Ask questions, seek answers, and try out various options.

SYMBOLISM:

- The Wheel of Fortune is a symbol of destiny and destination, of good luck and bad luck, of the ups and downs of life and fate. Everything is in motion, turning and floating, constantly changing, accidental and uncontrollable;

- In the midst of all this is suspended a wheel of ten spokes, according to the number of the Sephiroth, and of the sphere of Malkuth, indicating governance of physical affairs;

- Above, the firmament of stars. These appear distorted in shape, although they are balanced, some being brilliant and some dark. From them, through the firmament, issue lightning (indicating dynamic energy that is ever-evolving);

- On this wheel are three figures, the sworded Sphinx, Hermanubis, and Typhon; they symbolize the three forms of energy which govern the movement of phenomena;

- The sphinx unifies the four magic virtues: knowledge, will, daring, and silence. Wisdom arises through the unification of animal instincts and intuitive intellectual powers. The sword in the sphinx's paw testifies to the incorruptible powers of discrimination and the ability to think clearly;

- The ape on the left side of the wheel symbolizes flexibility (and looks as if he may be the one who keeps the wheel in constant motion);

- The crocodile represents the god of creativity (see also the Fool). It holds two tools: (1) the Ankh, a symbol of life, every creative act brings something to life; and (2) the staff with the hook at the end is a symbol of possibility we have to forge our own luck;

- The center of the wheel represents the sun, the absolute center which, despite constant movement at the periphery remains still and unchanged;

- The spokes of the wheel are equidistant from the center indicating that all paths are equally true, ending up at the same place. In short, in life there is nothing to win or lose, it's how you play the game;

- The triangle in the background symbolizes stability (as in 3 of disks);

- A mass of blue and violet plumes representing universal law, divine presence, royalty (as in "that which rules"); gold, reward, flexibility, malleability; yellow, spirit.

INTERPRETATION:

Everything revolves and is in a constant state of change. Nothing is static in life. Everything is either becoming or dying.

In Hindu philosophy, Tamas (darkness, inertia, sloth, ignorance, death), gives way to Rajas (energy, excitement, fire, brilliance, restlessness), which gives way to Sattvas (calm, intelligent, lucidity, beauty).

The trump also represents the need to be careful, to realize and recognize the vagaries of life, to accept the fact that fate is nothing what we could have done, but the result of what we already did. Today is the result of the past, future will be the sum of past and today, and no matter how accurately we plan, the Wheel of Fortune will mix up light and shadow.

Whether the Wheel of Fortune is positive or negative is not a matter of happenstance or events in the first place; but rather of the way we will deal with the results, arrange our lives with the unchangeable and work on what we might be able to change—and of course of our ability to realize facts.

Feeling lucky; experiencing providence; getting an unexpected surprise; finding opportunity in an accident; using what chance offers; benefitting from a happy coincidence; affected by synchronicities; feeling a sense of destiny; sensing the action of fate; seeing life's threads weave together; being at a turning point; reaching a crossroads; approaching a pivotal moment; feeling at the center of events; moving in a different direction; turning things around; having a change in fortune; altering the present course; being surprised at a turn of events; feeling movement; having the tempo of life speed up; being swept up in new developments; rejoining the world of activity; getting involved; having a personal vision; seeing how everything connects; becoming more aware; uncovering patterns and cycles; expanding your outlook; gaining greater perspective; discovering your role and purpose.

DIVINATION:

Change of fortune (This generally means good fortune because the fact of consultation implies anxiety or discontent).

Questions to ponder: Are you really ready for the great fortune? How can I best capitalize on the possibilities this situation offers me? How can I be prepared for inevitable vagaries of life?

Affirmation to give yourself: I am ready for the miracle of my life.

XI. LUST

TAROTNYMS

New and renewed purpose/burst of creativity/giving in to one's dreams/passions versus letting fears and rules keep one bound to old ways

Mastering one's animal nature versus letting one's animal nature rule

Surrender (unconditional devotion)/passion/love versus irrationality (lack of balance)/blind love/rose-colored glasses/unquestioning/without regard for consequences

Uninhibited expression of self versus disconnection from/inattention to others, selfishness

FOLLOWING YOUR BLISS

SNAPSHOT

PASSION/CREATIVITY/NEW (DESTRUCTION OF OLD)/RAW

BAUTA "HIDING PLACE" QUADRANT (SCOTT GROSSBERG):

The Mask: Passionate What makes me who I am; How I view myself; What I'm attracted to; What I take for granted in myself.	The Beast: Impulsive How others view me; What I excuse in myself; My deepest urge; What I resort to under stress.
The Shadow: Dull/Cautious The thing I have no wish to be; What I think I've left behind; What I become when all else fails; What I still must learn to control.	The Light: Focus What others think I need; What I look at with wonder; What I need for balance; What I desire to accomplish.

MEANING:

A card of passion and creativity, caught up in the moment. They like to think of themselves as having the joy of life, being uninhibited. Others will say she can be impulsive and lack depth, is distractible. When pushed, she can become dull and predictable, slow and plodding. To add balance, the person needs to stay focused, follow tasks to completion while maintaining passion.

Main Summary: Energy, passion, charisma, joy of life, the authenticity of the true self, shown in all its glory, being an uninhibited expression of life, no censorship of self, taming the ego, holding the reins in the receptive hand, holding the grail in the expressive hand, transmitting divine essence outward, loving life in all its aspects (especially love of self), celebrating authenticity, embracing passion for all things (beings), divine feminine in her unbridled beauty. Orgiastic experiencing independent of morality and limiting rationalism.

Bottom Line Interpretations (Tarantino): Excitement about the situation. Determination and enthusiasm give you the stamina to work through any obstacles and reach your goals. Follow your passion. Negative: avoid cynicism, rediscover your initial enthusiasm, or risk not having the staying power to be successful.

CORRESPONDENCES:

- *Number*: 11, primal force, inspiration, illumination
- *Hebrew*: 9, Tet, ⍨, Serpent
- *Positive*: Power, vitality, unconditional devotion
- *Negative*: Weakness, dissatisfaction, depression
- *Zodiac*: Leo (creative energy)
- *Planet*: Sun (pure energy), the primal force of the sun is being expressed within the confines of our human nature (the need for food, love, sex, touching, and all sensual and sexual experience)
- *Tree of life*: The connection between Chesed (Condensation/growth/stability) and Geburah (Movement/changing/destruction)
- *Element*: Fire
- *Life Themes*:

    "I am the sum of all my interests."
    "And they shall know me by move many loves."

- *Basic Divinatory Meaning*: (instruction booklet) Courage, strength, energy, use of magical power. Control of the life forces. Great love affair.
- *Advice*: Love conquers all. Avoid pettiness and prejudice. Try to be the peacemaker. Weigh all sides of every situation. Don't be so set in your ways that you miss the big picture by focusing on details. Stubbornness is your challenge of the moment. Alternately: everyone expects the best from you and vice-versa. Arguments with your love or close associates are likely now. Don't give in to intimidation or pressure, and never go to bed angry. Are you seeing things realistically? Wait one more day to take action.

SYMBOLISM:

- The woman is in a state of ecstasy indicating creative energy independent from reason and intellect. She's following (riding) her passions;
- In her left hand she holds the reins, representing the passion which unites them. In her right she holds aloft the cup, the Holy Grail aflame with love and death. In this cup are mingled the elements of the sacrament of the Aeon;
- Her head is turned completely toward the urn of fire. She is totally absorbed in the energy of transformation inherent in any total and conscious surrender;
- There is in this card a divine drunkenness or ecstasy. The woman is shown as more than a little drunk and as more than a little mad. The lion also is aflame with lust. This signifies that the type of energy described is of the primitive, creative order; it is completely independent of the criticism of reason;
- Seven heads on the beast:
    - The head of an angel;
    - The head of a saint;
    - The head of a poet;
    - The head of an adulterous woman;
    - The head of a man of valor;
    - The head of a satyr;
    - The head of a lion-serpent.
- Behind the figures of the beast and his bride are ten luminous rayed circles; they are the Sephiroth latent and not yet in order, for every new Aeon demands a new system of classification of the Universe. They represent the fading moral ideas which are now being replaced by fresh ones pulsating at the top of the picture;
- The new light emanating at the top streams out snake like in all directions to destroy the world and create it anew;
- At the top of the card is shown an emblem of the new light, with ten horns of the beast, which are serpents, sent forth in every direction to destroy and

re-create the world;

- The paws of the beast walk over images of the pious in prayer. This is not a time for reminders of what it is to feel shame, and they are relegated to the background, fading next to the vibrant colors that define beast, rider and chalice;
- The faces in the background with folded hands represent old fears and restrictive condition;
- The lion and the maiden represent the beauty that is within each of us. The radiant leonine energy can be tamed and put to beneficial use for all humanity, allowing the wielder to possess great strength, energy and use of magical power, shifting great oceans and lands beneath the footprints of the giants, who sleep no more and rise with a breath;
- The color orange/gold/red, represents vitality, life force, integrity; green, creative force.

INTERPRETATION:

In other decks, this trump is called "The Power," a symbol for the mastery of our own animal side. Crowley named the card 'Lust'—and most people don't really think of mastering their inner animal, but enjoy it full tilt.

In a combination of both, the animal side shouldn't be "mastered" in the meaning of "suppressed," nor should it be let out to "romp around." It should not be ignored, but accepted as a natural part of oneself. In that manner, one will not only be able to profit from its instinctive natural power, but also to save the power needed to "master" it.

The card implies vitality, energy and power. The card tells us to use these riches. In most aspects of life, an endeavor will have much more success when passion is put into it.

Lust implies not only strength, but the joy of strength exercised. It is vigor, and the rapture of vigor.

Love under will.

The appearance of Lust is going to indicate we are dealing with the realm of passion, energy and drive. In astrology, this card corresponds to Leo, and indicates going forth, of feeling things, of being moved. It may, indeed, represent sexual lust–the kind of desire that comes from deeply wanting another person, the kind of desire that will propel us forward to try harder, do more, and strive to do something spectacular to catch the attention of the person we crave. But it can also represent a more general "lust for life". Rather than meaning the kind of excitement we might feel when we wake up refreshed while on holiday and we feel ready to seize the day, this is the kind of deeply felt lust for life that comes from doing the thing you were born to do, from being at the place are meant to be, surrounded by *your* people.

In life we can play it safe, be careful, and not care too much about the things that cross our path. But if we do so we may find our life is dry, uninteresting and passionless. If, however, we allow everything to move us, everything to pull us one way or another, every slight raises anger and every affection turns to burning lust, we won't be bored, certainly, but we may find our life is constantly in chaos and we crash from one incident to another barely in control. We have to balance our passion with our will–our ability to feel, to love, to be moved with our ability to guide, judge and discriminate.

Balance of technique and emotion (e.g., in music).

DIVINATION:

Placed positively it indicates a great passion, finding the thing you are *supposed* to be doing in life, feeling a great, moving, lust or desire. Placed badly it may indicate that you are being ruled by your emotions, that you are being dragged hurtling forward by drives and desires you cannot control, that you have little hope but to hang on for dear life until this ride ends.

Let go and experience the fullness of this moment, reject nothing, accept all the present moment offers.

Questions to ponder: What areas of your life would you like to live out more fully? What has prevented you from doing so in the past? Are you willing to stay with it even when the odds seem stacked against you?

Affirmation to give yourself: I enjoy living to the utmost.

XII. THE HANGED MAN

TAROTNYMS

Stagnation and or a period of challenges and difficulties versus a turning point/time for a change

Needing to change versus need for status quo, stability and safety or unwillingness to look at the reality of the situation

Ability to endure (hanging on) versus fatalism/ inability to see the repetitive patterns that bind us

TRAPPED BY YOUR PATH

SNAPSHOT

STUCK/NEED TO BREAK THROUGH, MOVE ON/FATALISM WITH LOSS OF PERSPECTIVE/BLINDNESS/ TRANSMUTING POWER OF SPIRIT

BAUTA "HIDING PLACE" QUADRANT (SCOTT GROSSBERG):

The Mask: Sacrifice/Martydom What makes me who I am; How I view myself; What I'm attracted to; What I take for granted in myself.	The Beast: Victim How others view me; What I excuse in myself; My deepest urge; What I resort to under stress.
The Shadow: Predatory The thing I have no wish to be; What I think I've left behind; What I become when all else fails; What I still must learn to control.	The Light: Avenging/Proactive What others think I need; What I look at with wonder; What I need for balance; What I desire to accomplish.

MEANING:

Someone who sacrifices, feels s/he has no other choice than to take on/tolerate burdens, whims, and wants of others. Others likely view this person as a victim, the person pushed by circumstance. When pushed, the person can become downright mean, moving beyond being a victim, selfishly plundering those around her. To maintain balance, the person must abandon the principles for which s/he ordinarily suffers, becoming proactive, avenging rather than suffering in silence.

Main Summary: Enforced sacrifice, punishment, loss, fatal or voluntary, breaking of personal will, stalemate, suffering, defeat, failure, death, end of a situation or relationship that is stuck, necessity of breaking through old behavior patterns.

Bottom Line Interpretations (Tarantino): The situation is temporarily beyond your control. In this specific situation you may have to yield to overcome. You are at the initiation phase of an important transition. Negative: stop hitting your head against the wall. Try a new approach.

CORRESPONDENCES:

- *Number*: 12, the perfect number, symbol of the zodiac, 3 x 4, meaning surrender of the ego
- *Hebrew*: 40, Mem, מ, water
- *Positive*: Overcoming the ego, changing life, a new sight of the world
- *Negative*: Standstill, rejection, loss of perspective
- *Zodiac*: Pisces (the last of the signs, meaning sensitive)
- *Planet*: Neptune (sign of intuition, understanding, emotion)
- *Tree of life*: From Geburah (Movement/destruction) to Hod (Intellect/logic/structure)
- *Element*: Water
- *Life Themes*:

    "I am the sum of all my sacrifices."
    "And they will know me by my possessions."

- *Basic Divinatory Meaning*: (instruction booklet) Redemption through sacrifice. Enforced sacrifice. Suffering. The moment before transformation occurs. Ill-dignified: Punishment, loss defeat, failure, death.
- *Advice*: Rise above material concerns and the way things have always been. Try another avenue. Relax and rethink. Keep everything aboveboard. Allow others to change their minds and look at new options. Contemplate don't agitate. Alternately: Stop being so closed minded. There are plenty of alternatives and solutions to your problems. Try something new. This is no time to be lazy or melancholic.

SYMBOLISM:

- There is a lot of green on it: green disks sit at the end of each limb and under the head. Green is the color of Venus here signifying Grace, with a big "G", like the grace of God: the "freely given, unmerited love of God;"
- The disks are indicative of the earth, Malkuth, the realm of coins, and the suit of the tarot which refers to the physical body, its wants and needs, as well as possessions and material wealth;

- The man is hanged upside down representing that we must surrender our illusion of control, see life from another angle;
- The grid behind represents the structures that support him. He is being crucified on his own grid;
- The Hanged Man is suspended from an Ankh, the Egyptian hieroglyphic for "eternal life" and is nailed to the wood of his petrified attitudes and viewpoints;
- His eyes are closed as he is blind to all which does not fit into his closed system of concepts;
- His head is shaved. The hair, a symbol of spiritual perception, is removed. He's lost trust in his own intuition;
- His legs in the shape of number 4, the Emperor (stability/order), meaning we must give up the present order;
- The snake curled at his feet represents the possibility of transformation;
- The serpent of creation, transformation, and wisdom lays coiled and sleeping;
- The sun on the horizon means that a new day is coming;
- The color green symbolizes hope (creativity) that comes with surrender; blue wisdom (new ideas); black, depth of the unconscious.

INTERPRETATION:

The Hanged Man is a symbol for the turning points in life, showing up a need to stop and assess a situation. We're hanging in the air until we find a new view of the things around us, a proper way to rearrange or start.

The point is that you can no longer avoid seeing naked realities.

But the Hanged Man is a "silent." card—there's no pressing need for change. No big change is waltzing towards us—we can peacefully keep on hanging and complaining. The Hanged Man just shows that we're just "hanging," he requires a new viewpoint, and sometimes a lot of patience.

In its positive aspect, the card shows the need for a time of consideration, the forced relaxation gives the opportunity to relax and reflect, to sort thoughts and ideas and find a new way to cope with a situation.

The Hanged Man symbolizes the universal principle of recognizing and awakening ourselves to repetitive patterns that bind, limit and restrict our personal potential.

Self-surrender to higher wisdom. Waiting period. Complete reversal of affairs. New way of looking at life. Moving beyond limited consciousness. Breaking old patterns. Complete and unexpected change is looming. Salvation through sacrifice (make sacred). Loss of ego. I let go and realize. Follow and accept the will of the divine in my life that reveals itself to me step by step. Sacrifice of one thing for another. Ability to delay gratification (Draw another card to see what to surrender to).

Bowing willfully to the cosmic order of the Universe.

DIVINATION:

If the Hanged Man is prominent in a reading there is often a sense of fatalism, waiting for something to happen. Time has stopped and we are outside our lives looking in.

Hanged Man can often be the scariest challenge, because in terms of spiritual development it demands a willingness to turn your back on everything and everyone that defines your identity. You must be ready to drop the hard-won knowledge and wisdom which may well have also brought you reputation and respect, and all that makes you who you think you are. This is nothing less than the death of the ego.

Recognize that you are stuck. There is nothing to do, merely perceiving your reality clearly makes transformation possible. This is a time of initiation, when trust is needed, and surrender is called for.

Questions to ponder: In what areas of your life are you stuck? Are you ready to recognize and let go of your petrified thought and behavior patterns? In the name of progress, why are you so unwilling to try a new approach?

Affirmation to give yourself: I let go and realize, follow and accept the will of the divine (providence) n my life which reveals itself to me step by step.

XIII. DEATH

TAROTNYMS

Rebirthing and growing phase versus uncertainty/lack of familiarity/starting anew

Forced to make a change/adapting to change versus desparately clinging to old ways

Embracing the new versus caught in fear, loss, loneliness, uncertainty

Time for new ideas versus clinging to the old ways/traditionals which provide structure but no inspiration

KNOCKED OFF YOUR PATH

SNAPSHOT

END/EXTERNAL (IMPOSED) CHANGE (TRANSMUTING POWER OF NATURE)/RE-BIRTH

BAUTA "HIDING PLACE" QUADRANT (SCOTT GROSSBERG):

The Mask: New Born/External Change What makes me who I am; How I view myself; What I'm attracted to; What I take for granted in myself.	The Beast: Disenchanted How others view me; What I excuse in myself; My deepest urge; What I resort to under stress.
The Shadow: Entrenched The thing I have no wish to be; What I think I've left behind; What I become when all else fails; What I still must learn to control.	The Light: Enchanted What others think I need; What I look at with wonder; What I need for balance; What I desire to accomplish.

MEANING:

This card does not refer to physical death, but of re-birth, re-awakened consciousness, and change. The person is looking for an out, escape from a real or imagined situation. People around them will say they are disillusioned with life, and often disappointed. When pushed to the point where hope and expectation are no longer viable strategies, s/he becomes entrenched in the current life course. To achieve balance, the person needs to find charm, and delight both around and within.

Main Summary: Change, ending of something to make way for the new, coming to a conclusion, letting go of the past.

Bottom Line Interpretations (Tarantino): Everything is changing for the better, celebrate it. Cut to the core, keep what works, and dispose of everything else. These changes will allow you to revitalize yourself or situation. Negative: if you do not change, your situation will deteriorate. The circumstances surrounding this situation have been extremely painful so life is being kind to you by taking matters out of your hands and insisting that you let go. When resisted, transition can be a slow and painful process.

CORRESPONDENCES:

- *Number*: 13, the number destroying the perfection of the 12, back to basics
- *Hebrew*: 50, Nun, נ, fish
- *Positive*: Make place for something new, get rid of old loads and achieve new spaces
- *Negative*: Fear and loss
- *Zodiac*: Scorpio (dark, all consuming)
- *Planet*: Mars (aggression, hostility, destruction) and Pluto (transformation)
- *Tree of life*: The axis Tiphareth (Balance/middle/harmony) – Netzach (Creativity/sensitivity/anarchy)
- *Element*: Water
- *Life Themes*:

    "I am the sum of all the lives I once lived."
    "And they shall know me by my wisdom."

- *Basic Divinatory Meaning*: (instruction booklet) Transformation. Radical external change. Change voluntary or involuntary, perhaps sudden and unexpected. Apparent death or destruction that is illusory when viewed from a higher perspective.
- *Advice*: You are entering a growing phase. Acknowledgement comes slowly. No one will offer a helping hand unless you beg for it. Get rid of an old habit. Stop doing things that don't feel right for you. Setbacks and delays likely.

SYMBOLISM:

- The skeleton which alone survives the destructive power of time, may be regarded as the foundation upon which the structure is built, the type which persists through the permutations of time and space, adaptable to the requirements of evolution and yet radically unchanged, symbolizing down to the basics, the "bones of things." The skeleton is in the position of Saturn, doing the "dance of death," indicating continual transformation;

- The transmuting power of nature working from below upwards, as the Hanged Man is the transmuting power of the spirit working from above downwards;
- The colors are blue—green, both dark and pale, the two dominant colors of the visible world, and the flashing colors of orange and red-orange;
- The Death figure wears Osiris' helmet, linking it to the previous card. This is the resurrection—the Hanged Man has been through the agony, and now there is rebirth; the redemption, the salvation, the change had come to pass. Death is the ultimate operative of the natural cycle, destruction being the force in nature that paves way for the new. Change occurs in life, whether desired or not. This has to be met with acceptance. The helmet can also symbolize the need to take old ideas to the grave;
- Scorpion, representing primitive energy always ready to commit suicide when heavily beset but willing to undergo any transformation that will permit its continued existence;
- The blossoms of two lilies (water [emotion] and holy) lay dying in the mud, representing death and transformation;
- The onion, the necessity of peeling away layer after layer;
- Fish and serpent, signs of resurrection, the snake, transformation, the eagle soaring to new heights;
- Bubbles symbolize the positive and creative side of death;
- The figures emerging from the background represent potential new forms of life (ideas, relationships, possibilities, etc.).

INTERPRETATION:

The Death represents the never ending circle of death and rebirth as the precondition for new life and creation, for life is permanently changing, hello and good-bye, leaving and arriving.

The Death will show that something has ended and something will begin, and doesn't care if the end is painful and the new beginning welcomed or vice versa. The card implies the need to let something go, and requires the understanding of the circles of life.

The negative aspect of the card could plainly mean that we want to keep what we have to give up, that no change is welcomed. In most cases it is just a refusal to understand and accept. It can mean we are scared of loss and also afraid to restart.

Seldom does the appearance of this card signal physical death, but rather a dramatic, inevitable life change. While it may seem "out of control" this is more a return to one's original alignment. The idea of "what is death to the caterpillar is birth to the butterfly" a transition to a more appropriate way of being, a freedom in being released from ways that no longer work.

Old relationships demanding to be disintegrated. Everything one has believed in has failed, leaving nothing to hold onto. A new way of looking at things is required.

Death has two faces, one destroying, the other freeing one from old bonds which have become confining.

Any attempt to hold on or cling to old bonds will cause their death to appear that much more agonizing.

DIVINATION:

When Death appears it almost always signifies a major change in one's life. Sometimes the change will appear disruptive and unexpected, sometimes it will be a breath of fresh air—clearing away obstacles and allowing you to surge forward. So do not assume that Death is a negative card—it is often just what we need in order to progress when fear is holding us up.

Drawing this card generally means the person is ready for the change.

You will soon be presented with the opportunity to rebuild your life.

Death is related to Scorpio and the 8th house, which is about other people's money, secrets and sexuality. So, finding out about the sexual proclivities of someone is one interpretation. If you want to know what or where the secrets are, the cards around Death will give you a clue. The money, values and sexuality of our partner is indicated. If the Death card is surrounded by Disks cards, this is a generally a good sign of improving finances.

Questions to ponder: To what old relationships and situations is one clinging? Have I had enough of the status quo?

Affirmation to give yourself: Say now, yes to death, yes to myself and change.

XIV. ART

TAROTNYMS

A renewed purpose, direction, acceptance, creativity versus the need to overcome/unify polarities/opposites

Sense of balance and harmony versus some areas of life remain out of balance/inability to compromise

Potential for unity/resolution following conflict versus acting alone/difficulty trusting or unwillingness to compromise

Inner spiritual transformation versus out of balance or inattention to spiritual matters

Time for careful deliberation/mixing/measured action versus rash decisions/actions

PUTTING IT ALL TOGETHER

SNAPSHOT

INTEGRATION/SYNTHESIS/INNER AS OPPOSED TO OUTCOME/CHANGE/FULFILLMENT/PEACE

BAUTA "HIDING PLACE" QUADRANT (SCOTT GROSSBERG):

The Mask: Balanced	The Beast: Abstaining
What makes me who I am; How I view myself; What I'm attracted to; What I take for granted in myself.	How others view me; What I excuse in myself; My deepest urge; What I resort to under stress.
The Shadow: Indulged	The Light: Indulgent
The thing I have no wish to be; What I think I've left behind; What I become when all else fails; What I still must learn to control.	What others think I need; What I look at with wonder; What I need for balance; What I desire to accomplish.

Need to blend the right ingredients together in order to produce a balanced, non-stressful environment. Others view this person as someone who avoids excesses. Under stress, she engages in self-denial. Pushed past that point, s/he gives in to the trait despised in others, giving in to desire. To achieve balance, life should be embraced, including the "extras" and anomalies that heretofore signaled imbalance.

Main Summary: Integration, synthesis and synergy, combining forces, maintaining balance, unification of opposites, inner change (as opposed to external change from the prior card, XIII, Death), transformation, learning the lesson of the hanged man (which forces one to take on a new view), creative power, constantly bringing opposites into play in order to expand inner perspective.

Bottom Line Interpretations (Tarantino): Your life is full of possibilities but matters may not seem as clear cut as once thought. You may have to be patient before they materialize. A delay can only serve to benefit you. Negative: nothing seems to be working out as planned. To succeed, you may have to proceed in a totally different way. Will power will not get the results you desire. Try slowing down, avoiding extremes, compromising, negotiating, and moderation.

CORRESPONDENCES:

- *Number*: 14, as two times the 7, adjustment of destiny (reorganizing), new opportunities
- *Hebrew*: 60, Samekh, ⌂, lean upon, support, uphold, tent
- *Positive*: Balance and harmony, fulfillment, creation, peace
- *Negative*: Getting into extremes, splitting up and tearing apart
- *Zodiac*: Sagittarius, the archer (subtle energy, swift, light elusive)
- *Planet*: Jupiter (luck and expansion)
- *Tree of life*: From Yesod (reflection and imagination) to Tipareth (balance/middle, consciousness/harmony)
- *Element*: Fire
- *Life Themes*:

    "I am the sum of all the things I am allowed to embrace."
    "And they shall know me by my acceptance."

- *Basic Divinatory Meaning*: (from the instruction booklet) Combination of forces. Realization. Action based on accurate calculation. Economy. Management. Success after elaborate maneuvers. The way of escape.
- *Advice*: Compromise brings happiness. Try to see the other side of the story. Use common sense and good management. Those around you are playing to win. Don't be foolish or self-centered. There's lots of posturing in the air. Access favors and be kind but always listen to your higher self.

SYMBOLISM:

- Each symbol on the card represents the union of opposition, creating something new. This process is called synergy. You temper the flows of opposites by modifying the flavor, adding new components and bringing opposing parties together. It is this process of combining and re-combination that brings about the healing magic of creation;

- Fire and water merge to create steam. This metaphor is pictured with Leo the lion drinking from the cauldron with Scorpio, the eagle/phoenix, which is a water sign. They drink from the cauldron which contains air, the life force of the universe. The cauldron symbolizing that something new is brewing;
- On the cauldron is another union of polarity symbolized by the bird and skull (the union of life and death) which is a prevalent experience for ourselves as life and death are one in the same. Alternately, the raven sitting on the skull on the cauldron symbolizes death and life;
- The great sun disk unifies together with the crescent moons, from which the spinning stars are created;
- There is another significant message and that is of **Sagittarius** which is represented by the arrow shooting up the central axis of the figure of humankind. Sagittarius reminds us that through our life visions and dreams we fully express our unique artistry, while resolving any conflicts within ourselves;
- The red lion has become white, the white eagle has become red, symbolizing the transmuting of objects into their opposite;
- The black and white personages which were the lovers in card VI are now interchanged and fused;
- The rainbow symbolizes faith;
- Bees are a sign of industriousness;
- Green is the color of creativity, regeneration; orange, vitality; blue, wisdom, peace, harmony; aqua blue, intuition; white, clarity;
- Steam, new energy arises.

INTERPRETATION:

The Art represents the art of alchemy, the ability to solve and combine, to turn something plain into something precious.

The Art is the symbol for the right mixture, the perfect balance, standing for harmony, beauty and peace. But the trump can also show that sides that were previously ignored should be lived out and that contrasts should be put together to enrich the inner spectrum with new perspectives.

Okay, this is a time to come into quiet composure and maintain a calm air of deliberation, finding the energy of moderation and self-restraint. Climbing to the middle ground is important as this is the place where the calming air lives, the peace and tranquility in the eye of the hurricane where the beholder of the journey finds the important balance of self.

DIVINATION:

Perhaps the person is not viewing matters objectively.

Moderation and balance in all things. It is not a time for radical action or over-indulgence.

The others around you are more set in their ways now. Postpone debates and arguments until they can open their minds.

Questions to ponder: What do you desire at this time from the present situation? What do I need to mix into the equation to achieve success?

Affirmation to give yourself: My life is full of glorious possibilities.

XV. THE DEVIL

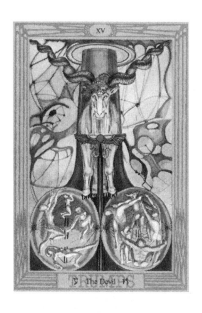

TAROTNYMS

Trailblazer, pioneer, adventurous versus outcast/lonely

Daring versus foolhardy/impulsive/safe

Independent/confident versus selfish/arrogant/proud

Embracing all of life versus loss of direction/indulgence or, in some instances, denial of physical pleasures and pursuits

DARING TO EMBRACE ALL OF LIFE

SNAPSHOT

FREE-WHEELING/EXPLORATION/
QUESTIONING/SEEING MORE/LIVING/
IMPULSE

BAUTA "HIDING PLACE" QUADRANT (SCOTT GROSSBERG):

The Mask: Free What makes me who I am; How I view myself; What I'm attracted to; What I take for granted in myself.	The Beast: Risky How others view me; What I excuse in myself; My deepest urge; What I resort to under stress.
The Shadow: Confined/Conservative The thing I have no wish to be; What I think I've left behind; What I become when all else fails; What I still must learn to control.	The Light: Thoughtful What others think I need; What I look at with wonder; What I need for balance; What I desire to accomplish.

MEANING:

Main Summary: The freedom of spirit, independence of mind, anarchy of science.

Bottom Line Interpretations (Tarantino): You are taking yourself and your situation way too seriously. There's nothing holding you back. Lighten up. Take time to go and play a little. Negative: you are in denial. Tell yourself the truth about what you are feeling and you'll know instinctively what you need to do next.

CORRESPONDENCES:

- *Number*: 15, as the number of the full moon, giving expression to shadow. The cross sum of 15 is 6 (!)
- *Hebrew*: 70, Ayin, ע, Eye
- *Positive*: Independence, willfulness, never accepting dogma, never bowing the head. "Non servam": I don't serve!

- *Negative*: Darkness, loneliness, being misunderstood and an outcast
- *Zodiac*: Capricorn (sign of duty, steadfast, persistent)
- *Planet*: Saturn (slow, heavy, obstinate)/Moon (inner, imagination, unconscious, reflective, illusive, emotion)
- *Tree of life*: From Tiphareth (Balance/middle, consciousness/harmony) to Hod (Intellect, logic, structure), against all dogma, never caring for rules, freely uncompromising and independent. There are no restrictions, no limitations, nothing is forbidden. The Devil is aware of the darkness; he knows all the shadows and will go on researching even at a high price.
- *Element*: Earth
- *Life Themes*:

    "I am the sum of all my passions."
    "And they shall know me by the risks I take."

- *Basic Divinatory Meaning*: (from the instruction book) Blind impulse, irresistibly strong and unscrupulous person. Ambition, temptation, obsession. Secret plan about to be executed, hard work, endurance. Aching discontent. Materialism. Fate.
- *Advice*: Matter overpowers mind. Desires rule. Beware your dark side. The pursuit of material or sensual pleasures may taint your ability to think clearly. Cleanse yourself of behaviors and habits that are doing you no good. Things may be unclear for you now. Don't let past issues cloud today's progress.

SYMBOLISM:

- The goat represents the impulse to reckless creation without any regard for result. The goat is also the scapegoat, labeled and shamed by those who don't understand and refuse to explore their own spiritual side. Spiraling horns are an emblem for perceiving and balancing "on the edge," hence growth and revolution. The smile represents humor as a way to push beyond acceptable boundaries. The third eye represents intuition, and tells us that we must see the infinite possibilities within our perceptions, thus the magic of creativity;
- Behind the goat, the tree of life pierces the heavens, also looks like a penis, meaning active energy;

- In front of the goat, the staff of Horus, symbol of creative energy;
- The Mars like pattern of lines represent the fiery material energy of creation;
- The rings at the top are of Saturn (slow, heavy, obstinate), or Set, the ass-headed god of the Egyptians, symbolizing the focus of intentions;
- The figures in the testicles as human impulses. They represent aspects of our humanness that have not been given expression. If these are kept in check then it means that we control our impulses. If not, we give into them. And although this can be good in some cases, it can also be bad;
- The figures are four female and four male figures representing creative energy;
- The sexual graphic depicts the moment when creativity is unrestrained. Electricity sparks in the background, and webs of creation and change are at their most primitive state. The spheres contain developing creations. This card represents creation and conception;
- The color pink/violet, represents compassion, understanding; purple/blue, wisdom and harmony; aqua blue, emotion, intuition; white, clarity; earth tones, physical world.

INTERPRETATION:

Another of those largely misunderstood cards, the Devil can represent that which bedevils us, and also "devil" people in our lives, but more to the point, it represents how we create our own chains, and use the shadow side of our souls (ego) to justify our repressions. The creative force is suppressed here, blocked by Saturn's rings, while the horned beast smirks at our self-created trap. The beast is in fact a neutral force, judging nothing, but affirming Crowley's basic tenet "Do what thou wilt is the whole of the Law."

It leads perfectly on from the Art card which taught you about acceptance and reconciling opposites, because the Devil takes you further beyond accepted morals and social judgments to embrace all of life and who you are fully and passionately, particularly, with reference to your body and sexuality. So often in the past spirituality has urged us to deny the physical, including the body, and abstain from sexual pleasure because it's supposedly wicked or sinful.

The Devil, however, encourages you to explore your physicality and your animal instincts; to own them, love them, and understand them.

Look at that cheeky goat face. It's as if he's saying, "Don't take your spiritual development or this human experience too seriously. Live a little, laugh a little." All people who see the essence of the word can be recognized by their marked sense of humor. Only ignorant people are deadly serious.

Finally, many people on a spiritual path will find themselves at some point being persecuted, condemned or abused because of their beliefs. You may even be accused of being evil or working with the powers of darkness. So if this is happening for you now, the Devil asks you to just smile enigmatically, adjust your jaunty wreath, and carry on enjoying yourself, because you know the truth and that's what really matters.

By identifying and accepting the darkness within we learn to discover that it is simply the dark side of our light.

The Devil, represents a concept that it is so subtle it is easily misunderstood. In fact the early Christians, so misunderstood this concept that it is now considered synonymous with evil.

To understand this card, one must be free of all popular moral and superstitious ideas.

DIVINATION:

There may be people who demonize you, make you out to be the devil. Meet them with humor and lightness. Accept what life gives you. Keep your feet on the ground.

Questions to ponder: Do you have some wish or desire you don't admit to? What am I afraid of happening if I express my true feelings?

Affirmation to give yourself: I am the master of my life.

XVI. THE TOWER

TAROTNYMS

Openness, accepting of change versus clinging to old ways/letting fear and tradition push us to maintain status quo

Breakthrough versus breakdown

Inner transformation versus chaos and uncertainty

New beginning/changing old ways versus blind destruction/insensitivity/aggression/fall from glory

Seeing the truth/reality as it is versus waiting until it's too late/clinging to old ways/giving up/the truth hurts

CRISIS/DESTRUCTION OF FAITH IN YOUR CHOSEN PATH

SNAPSHOT

INTERNAL CHANGE/SHATTERING OF ILLUSIONS (PERSONAL 'TOWER OF BABEL')/RENEWAL

BAUTA "HIDING PLACE" QUADRANT (SCOTT GROSSBERG):

The Mask: Crisis/Inner Change What makes me who I am; How I view myself; What I'm attracted to; What I take for granted in myself.	The Beast: Demoralized/Victim How others view me; What I excuse in myself; My deepest urge; What I resort to under stress.
The Shadow: Elite/Ivory Tower The thing I have no wish to be; What I think I've left behind; What I become when all else fails; What I still must learn to control.	The Light: Hope & Encouragement What others think I need; What I look at with wonder; What I need for balance; What I desire to accomplish.

MEANING:

Disruption, both minor and major, storm threatening on the horizon if not already causing a downpour. Despite the best of intentions and force of will the person feels their mortality and vulnerability. Despite the general state of affairs, the person may appear to thrive on the drama of it all. Stressed, the person becomes dispirited and depressed. Pushed further, and these feelings give way to a sense of being "the chosen one," elite and privileged.

Main Summary: Radical internal change (as opposed to Death [13]), Far reaching inner transformation, healing, the old is destroyed to make way for newer beginnings, spiritual renewal, self-knowledge. Examine ourselves to identify the things to which we are clinging that no longer serve us well.

Bottom Line Interpretations (Tarantino): The very foundation of this endeavor is crumbling. It's a blessing in disguise. If honest, you recognize that the circumstances surround this endeavor have never been good. Once leveled, you can go back to square one and start anew. Negative: at some level, you knew there was a problem but did nothing about it. To avoid misfortune, you need to get your head out of the clouds and plant your feet firmly on the ground. Selective seeing and hearing has complicated the matter. Consider the possibility of initiating damage control so that matters will not end with total destruction.

CORRESPONDENCES:

- *Number*: 16, 16 as 4 x 4: endurance/hardening, tests and challenges. But the cross sum is 7, indicating direction and momentum
- *Hebrew*: Peh, פ, 80, mouth (word, expression, fire-spitting)
- *Positive*: Sudden realization of the truth, the will to change old ways, to recreate life and start something new
- *Negative*: Blind destruction
- *Planet*: Mars (aggression, hostility and destruction, harmful actions and sudden troubles)
- *Tree of life*: The Axis Netzach (Creativity/sensitivity/anarchy)—Hod (Intellect, logic, structure)
- *Element*: Fire
- *Life Themes*:

    "I am the sum of all my failures."
    "And they will know me by my return."

- *Basic Divinatory Meaning*: (from the instruction booklet). Quarrel, combat, and danger. Ruin, destruction of plans or ambition. Sudden death. Escape from prison and all that entails.
- *Advice*: Everyone wants to be admired. Others embellish the truth, but what's necessary and real will prevail. Illusions will be shattered, enemies revealed. Don't be upset if things don't turn out as planned. Try to compromise and see other's points of view. Delays are inevitable. A fall from glory is likely. Meet opposition with compassion and sympathy.

SYMBOLISM:

- The Tower is a symbol of self, its endurance and destruction, an allusion to sudden, maybe shocking realizations that crushes old views and persuasions, maybe the view of the whole world;

- A Tower struck by lightning (from the heavens/God), with raging fires within and the top of the tower falling. There are four geometric figures falling, head-first, from the ruins, indicative of their rigid (limiting) perspectives. The four represent mind, emotion, earth, spirit. Through selective seeing and hearing we create a tower (consciousness) that is impervious to new ideas, therefore becoming brittle (susceptible to being the fuel of its own destruction);

- Eye of Horus illustrates awakened consciousness which sees reality as it is. It can also be seen as the eye of Shiva, which when opened, destroys everything in view, as human made structures are a stain on the pure truth;

- The dove and olive branch symbolize the compassion toward oneself and others which arises out of self-knowledge;

- The snake symbolizes what is created anew;

- At the bottom right, the jaws of Dis, belching flame at the root of the structure;

- The lion-serpent Abraxas (or Xnoubis) and the "Dove of Peace," represent two forms of desire: the will to live and the will to die. There is yet another layer in meaning here, as the former is the feminine and the latter is the masculine impulse. Some may see these two as in contradiction, but in all actuality, "the will to live" and the "will to die" are the inseparable. "Wife and husband" of all creation. Life and death are a single manifestation of all energy;

- The color red/orange symbolizes life force, strength, vitality; brown/black, material world, earth.

INTERPRETATION:

The area of relative security starts wavering, our tower then falls and with it the walls around us that have become too narrow. It is rarely the evil, but rather the necessary development we meet when there is a change.

The Tower shows us a basic fact of spiritual life: the power of the gods can strike unexpectedly to break down all the long-established patterns and assumptions that we have taken for granted for so long.

Sometimes our limited vision of reality blocks our understanding and perception of truth. We begin to believe that the Tower, which we have been building higher and higher in order to reach the Gods, is the only reality. A cataclysmic force is needed to destroy this fantasy so as to allow us to recognize the powers which surround us. When this happens we must react with hope, letting go of our fears. The highest truths can now be realized.

There are many aspects of the Tower that should remind us of the lessons to be learned within the Death card. All life is change. We can learn our lessons the easy way, by being open and accepting, or we can do things the hard way, clinging to things and ideas that no longer work for us. In that case, life will come along and, like a hurricane, batter us with the winds of change till we submit.

It is mostly about the universal principle of reconstruction and renovation and is often seen to mean that the questioner is a healer, restorer and renovator who aids in or is experiencing the breaking down of the self-absorbed individual self ("ego") and eliminating what is false, artificial and no longer of use to the progressive individual.

A breakthrough in self thought that shatters the old structures of belief. The deconstruction of self-definition necessary for enlightenment.

Emancipation from the prison of organized life.

DIVINATION:

On a Tower day, we need to examine ourselves to identify the things to which we are clinging that no longer serve us well. We need to be alert to the concepts life itself presents us with. Listen carefully for random symbols which will point you in the right direction.

When the Tower rules, it is possible that unexpected events will take place that you hadn't seen coming. If so, remember that to resist change is to deny life, and bear in mind that life is eventually going to win this battle anyhow, so lay back, relax and accept. And keep your sense of humor close at hand!

Sometimes we will be asked to take a blind leap of faith under the influence of the Tower. Remember this card signals breakthrough and extension, growth from experience, and self-trust. Whenever you are unsure about in your abilities to deal with things, remind yourself what you have already passed through in your life. There's a river of knowledge flowing through you already.

You are either in or are about to enter a process that will bring about an internal transformation. Whatever this transformation destroys will also bring about the new; allow this force to work powerfully for you.

Questions to ponder: What's really going on here? What can you do to turn this situation around? Are you ready to view yourself and life with new eyes?

Affirmation to give yourself: Everything that happens in my life is for the best.

XVII. THE STAR

TAROTNYMS

See, discover a higher purpose/guiding light/one's place in the universe versus being fooled/no pot of gold at the end of the rainbow

Hope/reaching for the stars versus unrealistic dreams

Balance of the spiritual, emotional, practical versus the need to see the beauty/possibility in the Universe despite any current difficulties

SEEING SOMETHING HIGHER

SNAPSHOT

HOPE/REBIRTH (RENEWAL)/
OPTIMISM/BALANCE/INTUITION
(EMOTIONAL UNDERSTANDING)

BAUTA "HIDING PLACE" QUADRANT (SCOTT GROSSBERG):

The Mask: Hopeful What makes me who I am; How I view myself; What I'm attracted to; What I take for granted in myself.	The Beast: Pollyannish How others view me; What I excuse in myself; My deepest urge; What I resort to under stress.
The Shadow: Depressed The thing I have no wish to be; What I think I've left behind; What I become when all else fails; What I still must learn to control.	The Light: Somber/Realistic What others think I need; What I look at with wonder; What I need for balance; What I desire to accomplish.

MEANING:

Hints and teases of the closeness of a desired event. Filled with the promises of tomorrow, while coping with the accent of today. The person prospers on hope and desire, is always looking at what might be. Where this person remains upbeat and cheerful, others see the need for caution. They will say this person is optimistic to a fault.

Main Summary: Inspiration, crystallization, self-recognition, radiating, clear vision, think 'star of Bethlehem,' trust in the self, connection to universal intelligence. Faith, hope, rebirth. Help will come when it is needed.

Bottom Line Interpretations (Tarantino): There's no one in the world that possesses your unique abilities and resources. Don't be afraid to express your hope, dreams, and visions. Do what you feel inspired to do. Negative: It's your lack of self-confidence, not circumstances, that is interfering with success. Don't hide in the shadows. Give yourself the same understanding and acceptance you extend toward others.

CORRESPONDENCES:

- *Number*: 17, as the number of hope, continuation, stability through change, expansion of the 7, cross sum is 8
- *Hebrew*: 80, Heh, ה, Window
- *Positive*: Creative hopes, optimism, trust
- *Negative*: Destructive hopes, illusions, lost in dreams
- *Zodiac*: Aquarius (freedom through discipline)
- *Planet*: Jupiter (luck and expansion)
- *Tree of life*: From Chokmah (Energy/creation) to Tiphareth (Balance/middle, consciousness/harmony)
- *Element*: Air
- *Life Themes*:

   "I am the sum of all my hopes and dreams."
   "And they shall know me by what and who I do not have."

- *Basic Divinatory Meaning*: (from the instruction book) Hope. Anticipation. A dreamer, committed to sharing his/her vision with others. Like the stars, this vision may flicker on and off. Error of judgment. Unrealistic, disappointment.
- *Advice*: You have a chance to start over in longstanding situation. Remain humble. You'll need imagination to come up with options for action now. Examine and evaluate carefully. Reach for the stars, something bigger.

SYMBOLISM:

- Every form of energy in the card is a spiral representing possibilities, the power of dreams. The spirals going into the gold cup exit the silver cup as rectilinear in shape, indicating that an illusion of straightness blinds humanity to the beauty of the universe;
- The crystallization of water represents insight and illumination;
- The gold cup is the eternal renewal of categories, the inexhaustible possibilities of existence. The silver cup is practical manifestation of dreams,

the difference in size indicating that dreams are always larger than reality;

- The nakedness of the female figure and her arm positions represent openness, receptivity. She is a dreamer, committed to sharing her vision with others. Like the stars, her vision may flicker on and off;
- The rose represents the fertile earth, the barren ground, the need to plant seeds from inspiration;
- The butterflies represent transformation, current views will change and become liberated from old conditioning;
- The color blue represents wisdom; pink/violet, love, caring; green, creativity.

INTERPRETATION:

After the crisis of the Tower comes the healing balm and influx of the highest light, only made possible by the preceding disintegration. The cracks are how the light gets in.

The Star is the trump of hope and trust, for the sensitive understanding of cosmic coherence, the intuition that everything is in balance and harmony. It is related to the Adjustment (the cross sum of 17 is 8), but while the Adjustment keeps the balance deliberately, the Star keeps it with feeling.

One of the most hopeful cards in the entire Tarot deck. Ruled by the sign Aquarius, it is an emblem of the unity of consciousness and all the things that stir humanity to oneness.

The Star adds up to eight. Numerologically, eight is a symbol for the balance we establish between our inner and outer realities once we discover the two are connected. The inner and outer worlds are exact replicas of each other.

The Star is the point in the initiation process where we find out that our worldly experience is a projected image of whatever is going on inside us.

The Star in a spread generally means that the questioner has faith, hope, and trust. With these three forces working inside them all things become possible no matter how difficult their situation appears to be at the moment. Knowing that they are creating their own experience they understand in the core of their being that they have the power to turn anything around.

In the same vein, they also know that, 'it's all good' and in divine order, which enables them to see that everything is exactly as it should be even when it doesn't look that way. There is a high level of acceptance with this card, the kind of acceptance that comes from knowing that every experience has a purpose and is connected to something much greater than what we can see in front of us.

DIVINATION:

You gain a more penetrating view into your potential.

This card always marks a turning point, where positive energy flows into life in a swift-running stream. All that is left for us to do is to open ourselves to the remarkable powers which are always present when this card appears.

The Star is also called the 'guiding light', and is taken as a symbol of the deep realization that the chosen way is the right one, that the end of this way will be a good one, and that there is perfect harmony between the psychical feeling and the physical doing.

The Star can also tell when there is a mistake, some error in our feeling, that the way we feel so sure about isn't quite right. This is what makes this trump so kind as even in its most negative aspect it just gives us a gentle warning.

Fear gives way to the workings of self, time to live in the moment.

A good, happy, productive, future.

Questions to ponder: What can I contribute? What are my hopes, dreams, and vision? What talents do I possess that I'm holding back or not seeing? What keeps me from communicating my ideas?

Affirmation to give yourself: My connection and creativity show me the way to realize my ideas.

XVIII. THE MOON

TAROTNYMS

Subconscious path to light and greater awareness versus attraction to activities that we might prefer to remain hidden

Wisdom from looking beneath the surface/facing one's fears/impulses versus arrogance/pride/blindness/stupidity (to venture out in the dark)

Depend on your intuition (beetle) versus wait until there's better light/likely to be deceived/things are not what they seem to be/need a guide

Guides appear to offer advice about how to find the "light" versus "If you meet the Buddha on the Road, Kill Him"/they can point the way but cannot take you there

KNOWING YOUR DARK SIDE

SNAPSHOT

UNCONSCIOUS (SHADOW)/
MYSTERY/ILLUSION/
CONFRONTATION WITH FEARS/
POTENTIAL OF DEEP SELF
KNOWLEDGE/WISDOM

BAUTA "HIDING PLACE" QUADRANT (SCOTT GROSSBERG):

The Mask: Deep What makes me who I am; How I view myself; What I'm attracted to; What I take for granted in myself.	The Beast: Mysterious How others view me; What I excuse in myself; My deepest urge; What I resort to under stress.
The Shadow: Superficial/Predictable The thing I have no wish to be; What I think I've left behind; What I become when all else fails; What I still must learn to control.	The Light: Grounded What others think I need; What I look at with wonder; What I need for balance; What I desire to accomplish.

MEANING:

Loves the unknown, using intuition, surprises, and the unexpected. Others may view her as mysterious, capricious, arbitrary, and unknowable. When pushed, this person becomes superficial, mechanical. To maintain balance, this person could be more forthright, clear, and grounded.

Main Summary: Final testing, wrong turns, illusion, falsehood, caution, darkness before light.

Bottom Line Interpretations (Tarantino): Postpone decisions until you can really see what's going on. Be mindful that there may be a hidden agenda. Like all cycles, this too shall pass. Admit to not having all the answers at the moment. Negative: one of the most difficult phases is over. A person (or unresolved issue) from the past may reappear. Tie up loose ends, and move on.

CORRESPONDENCES:

- *Number*: 18, as the return of the animal, cross sum is the 9, meaning completion

- *Hebrew*: Qof, ק, 100, back of the head
- *Positive*: Intuition, wisdom, maturity, deepest self-realization
- *Negative*: Illusion, hysteria, fear, rejection of reality
- *Zodiac*: Pisces, the last of the signs (sensitive)
- *Planet*: Moon (inner, imagination, unconscious, reflective, illusive, emotion)
- *Tree of life*: The connection from Netzach (Certainty/sensitivity/anarchy) to Malkuth (Root/origin)
- *Element*: Water
- *Life Themes*:

    "I am the sum of all my wonder."
    "And they shall know me by questions."

- *Basic Divinatory Meaning*: (from the instruction booklet) Illusion, deception, bewilderment, hysteria, madness, dreaminess, falsehood, voluntary change. The brink of an important change. This card is very sensitive to dignity.
- *Advice*: People are acting clannish. Don't join the crowd. Read between the lines. Your intuition is strong but you are still likely to be deceived. This is not the time to start anything new. Have patience. Need to confront your fears of the unknown, in particular our own physical mortality. Rely on your instincts. Stay connected to family, relationships, work and your body.

SYMBOLISM:

- The moon symbolizes the unconscious. Here is the waning moon and is the most universal of all planets, partaking of the highest and lowest. It falls between the Star (unconscious desire) and the Sun (conscious striving);
- Bloody "yods" (hands) falling down from the moon on the path toward the light;

- The sacred beetle bears the sun through the darkness of night and symbolizes that a new day will come and "this too shall pass;"
- At the bottom of the card, the lines and oscillating shapes are reminiscent of EEG lines during REM sleep, and symbolizing the ebb and flow of life;
- A stream tinged with blood flows between two barren mountains;
- On the hills are dark and sinister towers representing fear;
- On the threshold stand the jackal-headed god, Anibus, guides to the underworld. They hold the keys of Mercury, meaning communication with the unconscious; at their feet are the jackals waiting to devour those who have fallen by the way. They represent our animal instincts which, if we accept their help, will be our anchors to the physical world and our greatest ally in our search for immortality. If we panic, they will consume us. It is our physical life—our family, relationships, work, and our bodies in particular—that will call us back;
- The guarded entranceway represents the vagina, changeable, moist, shadowy, possessing an eerie attraction. New life can arise only by passing through this gate. The path to awareness leads us through unawareness.

INTERPRETATION:

There's another thing you need to keep your eyes open for with this card; not only does it indicate out-and-out deceit, but it also shows us where there is illusion or uncertainty. In moonlight, you notice that things look very different indeed than they do in daylight. The Moon has a habit of casting things and experiences in a different light. Things are not quite what they seem. This card shows things up that are not what they claim to be.

This card represents impure horror, hidden darkness which must be passed through before light can be reborn.

All superstition, dead tradition, and ancestral loathing that must be conquered to tread down the path toward light using limited, lower senses: touch, taste, and smell.

The Moon isn't the most comfortable trump. Although everybody likes to equate it with the mysteries, rarely someone really enjoys the look into their own abyss, where sometimes the unvarnished truth is not too pleasant.

Embarrassingly enough, the Moon tends to show up what we generally ignore, refuse to see, or even deny all the time. But the step has to be taken, for without facing up to darkness, we will never see the light.

Guides you find along the way may offer tempting promises but do not know any more about how to get to the light than you.

DIVINATION:

An increase in psychic ability (trust self/intuition rather than eyes).

Deception and self-illusion.

Difficulties/challenges on the journey ahead.

This too will pass, a transient experience leading to great inner growth, a necessary step on the path, confronting our shadow side.

Confrontation with old beliefs and superstitions.

There is danger of forgetting your true goal in the darkness.

Temptations and illusory perceptions lurk along the way ready to lead you down the garden path.

Deception, chaos and confusion can also work to a person's benefit, so if s/he does not want people to know what s/he is up to, the Moon is an excellent sign she will not be discovered. This card is good for spies, illusionists, stage magicians, politicians, and anyone else who do not want others to know what they are really doing.

"The darkest hour before the dawn", the brink of important change.

When prominent you know that nothing is as it seems, particularly when it concerns relationships. All logic is thrown out the window.

Questions to ponder: What are your blind spots? What might tempt you from your path? What illusions am I holding on to, frightened of? What can I wait to address until it is lighter?

Affirmation to give yourself: It's always darkest before the dawn. Say, "How splendid is the adventure."

XIX. THE SUN

TAROTNYMS

Rise up to, Success, achievement, triumph/freedom from dominance and jealousy versus shamelessness/burning too brightly/or not enjoying or recognizing what one has or has accomplished

Energy to throw one's self into life/health (recovery from illness) versus waiting for the sun will rise rather than seeking it out/finding the right context/burning out

Self-assurance versus ignoring other's needs/desires/sharing the bounty

No life without sun but the sun can also burn, scorch, kill (arrogance/vanity/too much pleasure)

SUCCESS ON YOUR PATH

SNAPSHOT

OPTIMISM/HAPPINESS/HEALTH/ENERGY/GENEROSITY

BAUTA "HIDING PLACE" QUADRANT (SCOTT GROSSBERG):

The Mask: Happiness What makes me who I am; How I view myself; What I'm attracted to; What I take for granted in myself.	The Beast: Euphoric How others view me; What I excuse in myself; My deepest urge; What I resort to under stress.
The Shadow: Miserable The thing I have no wish to be; What I think I've left behind; What I become when all else fails; What I still must learn to control.	The Light: Realistic What others think I need; What I look at with wonder; What I need for balance; What I desire to accomplish.

MEANING:

Happy with the current situation. Achievement of the desired goal is near. Seeks pleasure and avoids pain. Seeking happiness can be this person's narcotic. When stressed, anguish is avoided by becoming exaggeratedly joyful. Pushed too far, and unable to force happiness, the person takes on a pathetic and pitiful air, the very attributes s/he dislikes in others. To maintain balance, the person could be more concerned and realistic (critical or negative).

Main Summary: High creative energy, awareness, fulfilled love relationship, wisdom, happiness, success, achievement, confidence, self-reliance, good health.

Bottom Line Interpretations (Tarantino): Look for opportunities that open before you now and act on them. You've learned to trust yourself and your ability to accomplish what you put your mind to. It hasn't been easy. Prepare to reap the rewards of the day. Negative: you are doing much better than you thought. Of course, there are challenges to overcome, but now you can see them. Set realistic goals and get started.

CORRESPONDENCES:

- *Number*: 19 as a higher level of 9, the cross sum is 10 (> Wheel of Fortune > The Magician), meaning individuality, leadership
- *Hebrew*: Resh, ▨, 200, Head
- *Positive*: Vitality, generosity, warmth, self-confidence
- *Negative*: Arrogance, vanity, Sun as blinding, scorching, parching.
- *Planet*: Sun (primal energy)
- *Tree of life*: The axis Hod (Intellect/logic/structure) to Yesod (reflection and imagination)
- *Element*: Fire
- *Life Themes*:

  > "I am the sum of all my happiness."
  > "And they shall know me by my smile."

- *Basic Divinatory Meaning*: (from the instruction booklet) Glory, gain, riches, triumph, pleasure, frankness. Shamelessness. Recovery from sickness, but sometimes sudden death. Arrogance, vanity.
- *Advice*: Say what you feel when you feel it. Accept criticism and admit mistakes. Enthusiasm and self-assurance bring results. Don't get wrapped up in yourself so tightly you ignore other's needs. Stop being overly dramatic. Set goals realistically and try to do what is good for all involved.

SYMBOLISM:

- The green mound represents the fertile earth;
- The wall shows that the new Aeon (life, being) does not mean an absence of control;
- The twin children dancing outside the wall typify being playfully engaged in life, newly awakening energy. Their butterfly wings indicate complete freedom from restrictions and no longer wasted in struggles of dominance, jealousy, or boundaries as symbolized by the roses beneath their feet;
- In the center of the Sun blooms the rose of realization. Its light indicates

clarity and awareness;

- The zodiac signs represent the union of humanity, getting along with everyone;
- The Sun is the source of light (unlike the moon which merely reflects it), the symbol of life, for the power that always is generously given without reducing itself;
- The Sun stands for vitality and optimism, the blossoming of our nature, and is a sign that we have overcome the time of darkness and are ready to enjoy the light;
- Never forget that, without the depth of water, the sun will create a desert.

INTERPRETATION:

This is a warm, happy, energized card, which promises healing, growth and enjoyment—the most positive in the deck. We have emerged from the somewhat shadowy and mysterious realms of the Moon into the bright light of day now.

Gone are the tests and trials of our own growth, everything is here, there is no wished for goal off in the distance.

When the Sun shines, we find new ways of resolving problems, new perspectives and fresh viewpoints. We see things more clearly, and are able to objectively consider obstacles and difficulties. We have the energy we need to throw ourselves into life, and to dynamically deal with anything that we discover.

DIVINATION:

No matter what other cares and worries may weigh you down, on this day try to put them aside and simply revel in the glory of being alive. Today celebrate your victories, applaud your successes, and be proud of your achievements.

Any personal growth will be the result of self-expression.

The Sun indicates wealth, success, and happiness in the family. Look to the surrounding cards for where that wealth and success might come from. When weak, the Sun indicates the reversal of fortunes and problems in the family.

Questions to ponder: What task or project is on the agenda now? Are your goals realistic or are you expecting the impossible?

Affirmation to give yourself: I am in harmony with the divine light which shines in and through me.

XX. THE AEON (OR JUDGMENT)

TAROTNYMS

No parts, awareness of, acceptance of, belief in total, real self (good and bad) versus lack of awareness of true self/denying parts of self/insecurity

Identification/liberation of heretofore hidden abilities/life possibilities versus abilities remain hidden or subject to shame/non-acceptance

Setting off in a new direction/taking the first steps/make a unique contribution versus being self-important/being uncertain about self/indecisive

Redemption versus caught in old, self-defeating habits/beliefs/traditions

Body, mind and soul (shin) coming together to make a decision or set off in a new direction versus lack of integration of all parts of self

WHERE DO YOU GO FROM HERE?

SNAPSHOT

ASSESSMENT MERGED WITH ACCEPTANCE (JUDGEMENT)/RENEWAL AND REDEMPTION/BIRTH OF NEW SELF

BAUTA "HIDING PLACE" QUADRANT (SCOTT GROSSBERG):

The Mask: Assessment/Accountability What makes me who I am; How I view myself; What I'm attracted to; What I take for granted in myself.	The Beast: Resignation/Critical How others view me; What I excuse in myself; My deepest urge; What I resort to under stress.
The Shadow: Rejecting/Blaming The thing I have no wish to be; What I think I've left behind; What I become when all else fails; What I still must learn to control.	The Light: Accepting/Engaged What others think I need; What I look at with wonder; What I need for balance; What I desire to accomplish.

MEANING:

Pause to consider all that has been accomplished and all that has yet to be attained. This person values a discerning mind, prizing success and decisiveness. Others likely view this person as negative or critical. When stressed, this person can simply look resigned to his/her fate. Pushed to the limit, this person becomes obstinate, indecisive, rejecting, failing to take responsibility. To achieve balance, this person must remain engaged, accept responsibility and be judicious in assessment of self (balancing positive with negative).

Main Summary: Aeon is literally, "the new age," renewal, reassessment, receiving rewards due, acceptance of self (good and bad), the end of one period of life and the beginning of another.

Bottom Line Interpretations (Tarantino): Been given a second chance. Take responsibility for your actions and be willing to walk the talk. Keep your eyes open and mouth shut. Weigh any words before you speak. Negative: you've been afraid of making a mistake and so have made no choice at all. From now on, stop judging yourself so harshly and call your own shots. Accept responsibility for your current situation and it will improve dramatically.

CORRESPONDENCES:

- *Number*: 20 as 10 x 2 with the cross sum 2, the revelation of destiny, meaning choice
- *Hebrew*: Tooth, ש, Shin, 300
- *Positive*: Knowledge of coherences, widened perception and the liberation of hidden abilities.
- *Negative*: Wrong identification, self-deception, and megalomania.
- *Zodiac*: Aries (courageous, me first)
- *Planet*: Pluto (transformation)
- *Tree of life*: From Malkuth (Root/origin) to Hod (Intellect/logic/structure)
- *Element*: Fire
- *Basic Divinatory Meaning*: Birth, renewal, transformation, the realization of utopia. Final decision regarding the past. New current for the future. Always represents taking the first step.
- *Advice*: Job well done delivers many rewards. Laziness is punished. Make peace. Don't nit-pick one's self or others. Patience brings success. Health may improve but requires some effort. Desire to escape is strong. Listen, read all the fine print. Act now.

SYMBOLISM:

- In older decks the Aeon is called "Judgment," dealing with resurrection and redemption. The limitation of this view is the involuntary association with a "court of law," to the Christian concept of a "resurrection" where the pious may rise and the rest must burn;
- The Thoth deck veers away from the Christian overtones and instead we see the goddess Nuith, a primal sky goddess from the beginning of creation, symbolizing unlimited possibility. Her body is arched above our heads and curves to imply the ankh cross (resembling a uterus), a symbol of immortality, life, and unlimited possibility;
- The globe of fire is Hadit, standing for eternal energy.

- The union of unlimited possibility with energy is their child. A transparent male child figure stands within the ankh's loop with his finger to his lips in the traditional mystical gesture of silence. A seated regal figure is behind him. Both figures are said to represent Horus, first as child and then as ruler. The open hand is a symbol that the old universe has been destroyed but the new has not yet been made. His straight hair represents rational thought;

- Horus was the son of Osiris and Isis. When his father was murdered by his brother Set, Horus was protected and raised by Isis. Horus' ascension to manhood triggered a series of battles with Set, culminating in his assumption to the throne of Egypt. Set was sent away defeated and thus Horus is seen as a god of redemption;

- The birds represent new ideas;

- The fetus represents new life, rebirth;

- The letter Shin comes up from the bottom, is connected to the three figures meaning body, mind, and soul.

INTERPRETATION:

The Aeon is the trump of time and the changes dictated by the times, it addresses finality and destruction as well as liberation, hope and redemption.

The Aeon forces us to acknowledge that our actions set up a chain of cause-and-effect for which we are solely responsible. Here we pass through the fire of purification, shedding dead and dying wood as we go. We judge ourselves frankly, forgive, and leave the past behind. And then we are free to step into the light.

The final summation. All that you have been doing has led to this point. This is the moment where you say to the world "Here I am," and the world answers, "And here is the sum of your causes and effects." Kind of like Judgment, but more serene, the morning after.

DIVINATION:

The Aeon is another of those cards which indicate that we have reached a turning point, from this moment forward everything changes. There will often be big decisions to be made.

To improve circumstances, you must take full responsibility to follow through on your ideas and be willing to "walk the talk." Stop judging yourself by other people's standards.

Sometimes we'll find ourselves weary after struggling through a tough patch, but at the same time, now we see light at the end of the tunnel.

When we make life-changing decisions, we will often spend quite a long time thinking before we make up our minds. And during that period, we often berate ourselves for our indecisiveness and uncertainty.

When we do that, we are missing something so simple, and yet vitally important: that every decision we take has its moment. And if we are not sure now, perhaps that's because we have not yet reached this particular decision's moment in time. There will come a moment, if we are true to ourselves, when we know exactly what we need to do. And when that moment comes there will be no further prevarication, no doubt, and no fear.

When this card is thrown during a reading, the petitioner is usually experiencing a period of final decisions, judgment, and determination of an issue, and acceptance of results.

The petitioner is experiencing a natural progression of growth and maturation, where personal perceptions are dissolving to be replaced by a deeper understanding; a resurrection into a new stage of consciousness.

Spiritual truth is burning away, the falsehood of a man-made identity. The birth of a "new self" arising out of the destruction of the old self. Change of position, renewal, and outcome.

Insight cannot be arrived at by intellect alone, body, spirit, and soul must (the figures at the bottom of the picture) must enter the process.

Questions to ponder: What have you learned from past experiences? What do I know that I can apply in the present situation? Are you willing to wipe the slate clean and try again?

Affirmation to give yourself: The more that I know I don't know, the closer to the divine I am

XXI. THE UNIVERSE

TAROTNYMS

Free, peacefulness, independent versus the dependence on others/struggle to accept one's self

Enjoying the fruits of one's hard work and struggles versus needing to persevere and complete the tasks, end successfully/difficulty stopping to smell the roses, see everything happening

The spiritual (fire), intellectual (air), emotional (water), and physical (earth) are in balance/seeing things as they are versus the possibility of/need for a new transformation/direction (snake)

We see the endless possibilities before us versus being limited in vision/scared of the possibilities

FINISHING THE JOURNEY

SNAPSHOT

COMPLETION/SUCCESS/ATTAINMENT/WHOLENESS (AUTHENTICITY)/ENDLESS POSSIBILITY

BAUTA "HIDING PLACE" QUADRANT (SCOTT GROSSBERG):

The Mask: Satisfaction What makes me who I am; How I view myself; What I'm attracted to; What I take for granted in myself.	**The Beast:** Serene/Inactive How others view me; What I excuse in myself; My deepest urge; What I resort to under stress.
The Shadow: Impoverished/overwhelmed The thing I have no wish to be; What I think I've left behind; What I become when all else fails; What I still must learn to control.	**The Light:** Continued Development What others think I need; What I look at with wonder; What I need for balance; What I desire to accomplish.

MEANING:

Blissful and delighted by what has been accomplished. The person believes s/he can always rely on his/herself to provide exactly what is needed at the right time. Others can view the person as fortunate beyond imagination, satisfied to the point of inaction, or overwhelmed by the possibilities. When stressed, this person can retreat into daydreams and inaction. At worst, they can feel impoverished--despite how fortunate they are—or fickle.

Main Summary: The completion of a cycle of experience. A sign of success and attainment. Liberation. The person can enjoy his or her time of worldly success and fulfillment before starting a new cycle with new goals and challenges.

Bottom Line Interpretations (Tarantino): Be patient with the situation in question because it is one that will evolve and develop. Progress may not be linear and will likely involve trial and error. Stay committed to your goals and course and you'll get the outcome you want. Negative: don't expect the situation to resolve quickly. Be careful not to rush ahead without first establishing a step-by-step course of action. Until you are clear about your priorities, you'll be overwhelmed by the possibilities. The situation calls for self-discipline, structure, and tenacity.

CORRESPONDENCES:

- *Number*: 21, 21 as the symbol of the whole, 3 x 7, the cross sum is the 3, meaning creativity, possibility
- *Hebrew*: Tau, ת, meaning cross, 400
- *Positive*: Eternity and completion, harmony between spirit and body. Being home in one's self, inner independence, the "mental paradise"
- *Negative*: In its negative aspect the trump can tell us that we are running after false ideas, that our way leads nowhere, that it is far too early to reach out for the Universe for there's substantial work that has yet to be done
- *Zodiac*: Capricorn (sign of duty)/Aquarius (freedom through discipline)
- *Planet*: Saturn (Time of Harvest)
- *Tree of life*: From Malkuth (Root/origin) to Yesod (Reflection/imagination)
- *Element*: Earth
- *Basic Divinatory Meaning*: (from the instruction booklet). The essence of the question itself. Synthesis. The end of the matter. Delay. Opposition. Inertia. Perseverance. Patience. The crystallization of the whole matter. It is now possible to see things as they really are.
- *Advice*: Look at all side of the situation and surround yourself with people who love you. Refuse to be shaken when others try and undermine your confidence. Rewards are just around the corner. Don't give up anything to anyone. Seek intimacy and personal happiness in all you do.

SYMBOLISM:

- The sickle cuts away the old;
- The serpent of transformation, regeneration;
- The circle with a square indicates freedom through discipline;
- The gridwork symbolizes using one's limitations to grow;

- A maiden manipulates in her hands the radiant spiral force, negative and positive. Her headdress represents the evolution of consciousness. Her legs in the shape of a four indicates stability and balance;
- In the four corners are cherubim, symbolizing the established universe and the four fixed signs of the Zodiac (Leo, Taurus, Aquarius and Scorpio), related to the four elements (fire, earth, air, water). Contrary to their appearance in the Heirophant, here they are not ossified, but filled with new life;
- The skeleton house at the bottom is the building plan of the house of matter;
- The wheel surrounding the figure is the wheel of life which embodies the eternal becoming and passing.

INTERPRETATION:

The last card that started a cycle with the fool. (The Fool and the Universe together mean essence, beginning and end).

The great task has been brought to completion.

The world is seen as it is, all garments and masks become superfluous because you are at one with your original nature.

You are whirling, caught up in perpetual dancing motion of the universe.

The Universe as the end and completion of the Major Arcana is the symbol for the zenith of development—the achieved goal. The work is done or will soon be and we have found our place in life (or will soon do so).

Seeing the second decade of the Major Arcana as a way of self-realization, the Universe becomes the crown and the end. The Death was the rebirth, the Art the beginning of the alchemic work, the Devil the overcoming of restrictions, the Tower the breakdown of the jail. We followed the Star, explored the Moon, found the Sun and watched the Phoenix rise from the ashes. Finally, we touched the Universe.

Anything we choose to create begins with will and intent which triggers emotion, which drives us to think, which causes us to act.

DIVINATION:

On a more practical level the Universe implies the good news that a goal has been achieved, or a success sure to come, and that a venture will flourish.

Be patient. It may feel as though you take one step forward and two steps back. In the long run, everything moves forward.

Keep your plan in mind as you move forward. If you don't have a plan, first establish a step-by-step blueprint.

Once you are on track it will seem as if the Universe is providing you with the opportunities you need.

Questions to ponder: From what aspects of your life is it now time to free yourself?

Affirmation to give yourself: I am one with the universe.

8: THE MINOR ARCANA

THE FOUR SUITS

Fire	Water	Air	Earth
(active)	(passive)	(active)	(passive)
The Wands	The Cups	The Swords	The Disks
THE WILL	EMOTIONS	THOUGHTS	DEEDS
MAN	WOMAN	CHILD	FAMILY

WANDS:

Fire signs: Aries (3.21-4.19), Leo (7.23-8.22), and Sagittarius (11.22-12.21)

CUPS:

Water signs: Cancer (6.21-7.22), Scorpio (10.23-11.21), and Pisces (2.19-3.20)

SWORDS:

Air signs: Libra (9.23-10.22), Aquarius (1.20-2.18), and Gemini (5.21-6.20)

DISKS:

Earth signs: Capricorn (12.22-1.19), Taurus (4.20-5.20), and Virgo (8.23-9.22)

WANDS:

The element of the fire, standing for the spiritual, for creativity, mysticism, imagination (world of Atziluth);

Stands for energy in general, yang aspect, energy, perception, intuition, insight, activity.

The element of Fire is pure spirit; it is vitality and passion, energy and victory, the will and the power to act. It can mean pride and honor but also brutality and destruction. It is the gentle warmth and the soft light but also the terrible eruption of a volcano. The Sun as the ultimate symbol of fire is a life-giver and was adored as such since times immemorial, but the heat of the Sun could be a cruel murderer if it burned too hot.

Fire is the energy of heat and light, chemically a combustion reaction. It springs up fast and can burn wild and bright, yet it needs fuel to keep going. It is generally seen as the strongest and most powerful element but also as the one with the least endurance. Being seen in the fiery firmament as well as in the bowels of earth fire is both the highest and lowest element, given its archaic character it is both the most noble and the most primitive.

Humankind had been fascinated with fire ever since, watching it with awe and caution. Fire was about the most important precondition for man to rise from the level of animals, it provided means to cook and to have a light in the night, it enabled man to forge metal and build up a civilization.

One of the four classical elements, the old Greeks differentiated between the destructive Fire (Aidêlon) connected to the god of the underworld, Hades, and the creative, benevolent Fire (Aidês) connected to Hephaistos, the god of the blacksmiths and craftsmen.

In alchemy, fire is associated with Sulphur, one of Paracelsus' 'Tria Prima' (Three Primes). Metal is formed by fire in the womb of the earth.

In the Kabbalah, fire is the element connected to Chiah, the highest level of the soul, and to the world of Atziluth which is closest to the infinite. On this level, fire emanates (i.e. flows out from the pure white light of the infinite). It is thus seen as the divine spirit, the primeval spark of life itself.

In Tarot, the element of Fire is associated to the Suit of Wands, again stressing its importance for creation and alchemy, when the wand is a ceremonial staff, a scepter and thus a symbol of power. A cynic might note that a wand also resembles a club, yet another symbol for the hot and choleric temper of a fiery and unrestrained character.

ACE OF WANDS

TAROTNYMS

All blocks are removed (or about to be removed)/now is the time versus procrastinating/waiting for a better time

Courage to take action/energy available versus lack of focus/dissipation/must face difficult decisions about what to leave behind

A tremendous opportunity for growth awaits us versus fear about the future

ELEMENTAL SNAPSHOT

THE FLAMES OF INSPIRATION (ENERGY WITHIN)

MAIN SUMMARY MEANING:

The root of the powers of fire, energy, strength, pure, unadulterated, force, sexual vigor. The Ace of Wands is a symbol of spiritual self-realization, awakening, and is associated with the principle of truth and authenticity.

SYMBOLISM:

- A huge flaming torch, the second highest energy card (after the sun) in the deck, symbolizing the uncontainable life-force that's within. The green lightning bolts are a symbol of raw energy, capable of constant renewal, awakening to the spiritual truth and authenticity of who you are. The bursts of light (energy) go in all directions.

DIVINATION:

The starting of something worthwhile, good prospects, creative energy, enthusiasm. Can also mean that all certainties and security will be shaken or destroyed by the energies breaking forth.

Bottom Line Interpretations (Tarantino): You are on fire, your artistic juices flowing. Anything is possible if you're willing to get into the game. Negative: you need to feel excited and ambitious but are not. If you are not able to look at things honestly, it will be difficult to succeed. Don't rush, back off until you have a better idea what's going on.

Advice: Find a creative outlet. You can use the energy only if you have a goal to direct it toward. After releasing any blocks, find the right framework to set this energy to work.

TWO OF WANDS: DOMINION

TAROTNYMS

A strong, almost uncontrollable feeling of energy and passion pushing one to jump in, take on or take over versus needing to think things through carefully, consider the consequences/goal

Able to stand up/assert one's self and needs versus engaging in disputes and power struggles with no clear end (goal) in mind

Willing to give one's all versus being too idealistic or unable to see matters from others' perspective

ELEMENTAL SNAPSHOT

THE FLAMES OF WILL (ENERGY EXPRESSED)

MAIN SUMMARY MEANING:

Dominion. The card represents will, in its purest and highest form, without purpose or lust for a particular result. Energy. Fierceness. The crossing of action with new ways and methods, jumping head first at everything. When wrongly energized, it can mean restlessness, obstinacy.

SYMBOLISM:

- Zodiac = Aries (courageous, me first); Planet = Mars (aggression and power);
- The two crossed wands are "dorjes," the Tibetan symbol of the thunderclap, representing will and the initiation of action. The masks with the horse's

heads at the ends of the wands are symbols of pure destructive energy. The arrowheads are ornamented with snakes, indicating renewal or a poisonous bite. Six flames dart out of the center indicating energy and strength, but also uncontrolled passion and destructive tendencies (which is necessary in any act of creation). The blue color in the background represents air (ideas).

DIVINATION:

A need to be in command of one's self so that energy may be concentrated to provide the courage necessary to embark on new paths. A drive forward will result in finding new directions. Whatever drastic changes may occur, the pioneer will not be thrown off balance. Accept differences and apparent conflicts and solutions will become possible.

Bottom Line Interpretations (Tarantino): You need to act assertively if you are going to succeed. Let your ambition fuel your actions. Don't look to others for help. Trust your insights and creativity. At the same time, don't force it; work with the natural flow toward the results you desire. Negative: your doubts about your ability are undermining your power to act. Until you are fully committed the resources you need will elude you. Desire to reach your goal is important but must be accompanied by hard work and determination.

Advice: Work at staying centered.

THREE OF WANDS: VIRTUE

TAROTNYMS

Goodness, kindness and charity versus temptations/possibilities exist to violate one's sense of right and wrong/be selfish/cruel

Body, intellect, spirit in harmony versus one or more elements not in harmony

Harmony exists between inner wishes and external experience versus knowing one's desires but not matching external realities

Confidence/security/creativity versus pride, arrogance, conceit.

Clarity with regard to goals/desires versus must think about what one wants/desire/external realities prime for action

ELEMENTAL SNAPSHOT

THE FLAMES OF DEVELOPMENT (ENERGY DIRECTED)

MAIN SUMMARY MEANING:

Virtue, vitality, balance. Success after struggle. Pride. Realization of hope. Potential arrogance or conceit.

SYMBOLISM:

- Zodiac = Aries (courageous, me first); Planet = Sun (pure energy);

- Three golden wands with lotuses that are beginning to open are crossed through the rays of the sun's fire, symbolizing springtime, the generative energy that gets things going. Body, intellect, and spirit are in harmony. The flames form a five pointed white star, representing the basis of creative energy and signifying that each of us is unique. The restless free spirit of the Two of Wands (dominion), chasing nature out of lethargic winter sleep, is transformed into a powerful spring sun. The orange color symbolizes a sense of vitality.

DIVINATION:

A new sense of self-confidence comes into being and guards against an overload of unnecessary problems. Inner balance where we are clear about the things we want to create in our lives, and confident in our ability to make our dreams come true. Out of this clarity and confidence arises a new quality of self-reliance and happiness.

Bottom Line Interpretations (Tarantino): It's an extremely creative and fertile period for you. Be courageous and assertive. You are being encouraged to move into the situations you've felt insecure about in the past. Don't restrict yourself to the present area of exploration. Broaden your horizons. Expand your venture to encompass the full scope of your talents and abilities. Figure out what needs to be done and create a network of like-minded people willing to help you do it. Negative: back up and re-evaluate your situation before moving forward. Examine why your energy is slow low despite the presence of many opportunities to move forward. Maybe it's a good time to enjoy some rest and relaxation. Summer is just around the corner. No need to prepare as yet for the fall.

Advice: Cast aside doubts and fears, refusing to fall back into old habits. Instead you must turn your face to the future, trusting in your own power, making no compromises. Trust yourself, and everything else will fall into place.

FOUR OF WANDS: COMPLETION

TAROTNYMS

A sense of order (structure)/fulfillment/centeredness in life/pursuits versus senselessness/purposelessness/boredom

Accomplishing one's goals/work/spiritual pursuits/purpose/mastery versus feeling hemmed in/needing more structure/order

The right order is established/an injustice set right versus an injustice/order needing to be set right

ELEMENTAL SNAPSHOT

THE FLAME EMERGING INTO BEING (ENERGY CONTROLLED)

MAIN SUMMARY MEANING:

Completion, settlement, perfection, rest. Subtlety, cleverness.

SYMBOLISM:

- Zodiac = Aries (courageous, me first); Venus = beauty and love;
- The four wands have a ram on the top and a dove on the bottom. They cross through fire, forming what appears to be a wheel. The circle denotes completion, and the fact that life moves on. The dove symbolizes the finishing of something we have cared deeply about and now our energy is free to move into the next adventure (ram).

DIVINATION:

Knowledge brings conclusions, past efforts, rewards. The heart pushes forth and seeks the development of the beautiful in new directions.

The fulfilment of earlier hopes, ideas and dreams. The balance aspect, combined with the overall morality of Wands, brings us to think about injustice being resolved, inequity acknowledged and set right.

Tensions in relationships can work positively when the individuality of each partner is recognized and respected. Something beautiful is making its way into your relationships.

Bottom Line Interpretations (Tarantino): You've built a strong foundation. A successful completion of the task is in sight. Keep the momentum going by taking one step at a time and you'll achieve the goal. Favorable completion will give you the confidence to further develop the undertaking in question. Acknowledge and celebrate your achievements. Negative: at this moment, you seem to be caught in a conflict, wanting to move ahead but feeling trapped at the same time. Stop dragging your feet. It is crucial to finish what you start. To regain momentum, begin by taking one step at a time.

Advice: Question established conditions in relationships. Beware on guard for unreliable outcomes and overzealous action. Be tactful and gentle.

The inner, and more complex, matter that this card rules is that of the establishment of right order. When things are balanced in life, they flow more easily. When apparently contradictory forces come into equilibrium, the powers inherent in each is available to be utilized to their fullest degree.

As a result, when this state of balance is achieved, we become very effective in any area to which we apply ourselves. There is no time-wasting inner conflict, nor indecision. We can simply direct our energies in a single minded and competent fashion.

FIVE OF WANDS: STRIFE

TAROTNYMS

Full of energy (fire)/readiness/creativity but feeling blocked/meeting obstacles unfulfilled

Prepared/ready to compete (job/relationship) but transformation/creativity stifled/outlet blocked by circumstances/others

Challenge versus impulsiveness/recklessness

Awakening of one's own person/drives/desires/ambitions but frustrated in expression

Met by stiff competition that requires persistence and helps sharpen one's ability verses causes one to take reckless impulsive action

ELEMENTAL SNAPSHOT

THE FLAMES OF DISPUTE (ENERGY BLOCKED)

MAIN SUMMARY MEANING:

Restriction. Unfulfilled desire. Embittered, fearful, vain striving. Creative power is blocked. Challenges, obstacles, and competition.

SYMBOLISM:

- Zodiac = Leo (creative energy); Planet = Saturn (slow, heavy, obstinate);
- The center star is covered by overlapping wands, indicating our creative energy (Leo) is blocked (Saturn). The phoenix heads are turned away from each other, indicating that the possibility of renewal and transformation is also being thwarted. The yellow symbolizes the intellect trying to break through. Tiny wings at the bottom of the staff struggle to keep the heavy (leaden) wand afloat. The flames behind the wand burn with energy despite the current impediments indicating that, while currently frustrated, creative energy will eventually break through.

DIVINATION:

Problems will be experienced in the workplace, and they sometimes indicate that we feel overwhelmed by the number of tasks that we need to get through. There is, perhaps, a clash of personality with somebody else; or perhaps the individual is unhappy with working practices. Often in this situation there's a tendency toward rashness and loss of control which can lead to further problems.

Strife can also indicate inner conflict—most often about something we consider to be immoral. This is probably the most significant type of problem that can be highlighted with this card. For instance, if we have taken an easy option, or a dishonest turn, and are now troubled by the voice of our conscience, Strife can appear. In this case we need to set right whatever we believe we have done wrong.

Bottom Line Interpretations (Tarantino): Frustration with this project/situation is only temporary. It can be frustrating when things don't go as planned. Don't quit now. Step back if needs be to gain perspective. Negative: you've come a long way in handling the frustration over this situation. Remember, the path to your goal is not always a straight line. You must adapt to overcome. From this point on, it will be easier to maintain a steady flow of creative ideas.

Advice: Take things step by step, otherwise there is a danger of giving up. Courage, persistence and patience are required at this time. The card contains the possibility of transformation.

SIX OF WANDS: VICTORY

TAROTNYMS

Breakthrough after struggle/overcoming obstacles versus unhelpful influences continue to thwart dreams, hopes, ambitions, needs

Being gracious in victory/recognizing the role of chance/luck versus vainglorious/egotistical/power go to head

Success in conflict/competition versus left over pain and confusion from the struggle/fight

Time to enjoy peace/fruits of one's labor versus feeling embittered/let down by the fight

Period of stable and flowing/abundant energy/inner strength versus any peace is temporary/the price of peace is vigilance

ELEMENTAL SNAPSHOT

THE FLAMES OF LIGHT (ENERGY SUCCESS)

MAIN SUMMARY MEANING:

Victory, success, clarity, breakthrough. A card of fight, competition and eventual victory. It applies to areas of our lives where we feel we have had to fight very hard to achieve our goals. It can apply to any area of our lives where we have had to contest our position strongly. There will always have been struggle before this card appears. We will have been striving--sometimes against frustratingly unhelpful influences—to grasp our dreams, our hopes, our ambitions, our needs. There will sometimes have been pain or confusion as a result of that struggle. But when this card comes up, we can relax a little, and enjoy the fruits of our labor.

SYMBOLISM:

- Zodiac = Leo (creative energy); Planet = Jupiter (luck and expansion);
- The six wands are facing each other, harmoniously arranged and unified, strengthening each other: lotus blossoms, love; phoenix heads, rebirth or renewal; Eye of Horus with snakes, creative power. The nine flames burn steadily, lighting the way to success. Purple is the color of victory/royalty (endurance).

DIVINATION:

All goals will be reached. A phase of triumph and potential public recognition.

Bottom Line Interpretations (Tarantino): You are on the way to achieving your goals. The struggles that have plagued you will/are come/coming to an end. It brings particular satisfaction as your attainments are in line with your values. If you rely on your integrity, virtue, and principles, you'll experience both outer success and inner victory. Negative: victory may be elusive unless you stop questioning your talent, dig in, and give it your best shot. Any delays should be seen as an opportunity for self-discovery.

Advice: Use fair means and do service for others. Enjoy the feeling of success after a long struggle.

SEVEN OF WANDS: VALOUR

TAROTNYMS

Standing up for one's beliefs, values, needs (often without support/alone) versus indecisiveness, waiting to act "going along to get along," sacrificing self

Doing the right thing despite the odds/costs to current order versus feeling reluctant to challenge the status quo

Challenged to rise above one's self versus resigning one's self to fate

ELEMENTAL SNAPSHOT

THE FLAMES OF BOLDNESS
(ENERGY DEFENDING)

MAIN SUMMARY MEANING:

Honor, struggle, small victories. Intensification. Courage to meet obstacles. Prior equilibrium (and connection) is deteriorated. Victory will result only by individual valor (symbolized by the crude staff at the center).

SYMBOLISM:

- Zodiac = Leo (creative energy); Planet = Mars (male, warlike, aggression and power);

- The six wands are symbols for energy, united with the staff at the center, symbolizing a goal. The flames are disordered, indicating weakened energy and chaos. The large roughhewn wand in the center symbolizes the individual character and struggle required to meet objectives. The purple background is dark, denoting the courage that will be needed to move forward, the strong convictions one must have.

DIVINATION:

A card about encountering demanding and formidable situations in life, and having the courage to be true to your own desires, ambitions and needs. You may find yourself in a position where you are forced to fight for what you believe in. While sometimes reluctant to take up the fight, you will feel compelled to stand up and be counted.

Bottom Line Interpretations (Tarantino): Abandon any plan to maintain a neutral position. Standing up for your beliefs is going to take courage and audacity. You will have to fight for what you want. Look any fears in the face until they back down. Negative: you are allowing fear and anxiety to control your life. Don't be so quick to abandon your dreams. Have the courage of your convictions and settle for nothing less than the fulfilment of your vision. You have more to gain than lose.

Advice: Stand your ground. If you encounter resistance of any sort, remember that this card is about being true to yourself, following the voice of your own heart, and protecting your needs and hopes.

EIGHT OF WANDS: SWIFTNESS

TAROTNYMS

Development and progress at a rapid pace versus hastiness and superficial, tendency to be swept away

Sudden ideas and flashes of inspiration inundate/explode previous habits of thoughts versus difficult to form into a systematic whole/become reality

Resolving conflicts/longstanding problems versus tendency to hesitate/mistrust new ideas or energy/resignation

ELEMENTAL SNAPSHOT

THE FLAME OF IDEAS (NEW ENERGY)

MAIN SUMMARY MEANING:

Energy of high velocity. Activity. Approaching goals. Boldness. Freedom. Swift communication. Overcoming misunderstanding or blockages in our way.

SYMBOLISM:

- Zodiac = Sagittarius (subtle energy); Planet = Mercury (will and swiftness);
- The square in the center represents blockages/limitations which are overcome with energy transforming them into a crystal (three dimensional octahedron symbolizing midpoint between earthly (square) and divine (sphere);
- The rainbow is a symbol of wholeness, indicating that problems are coming to an end. Looking back, you can see how the difficulties have helped bring the learning process to completion.

DIVINATION:

The 8 of Wands always brings a new surge of energy and freshness when it appears. A problem which has seemed insurmountable recedes into the background because of new clarity. Everything is moving forward. Often it signals entry into a new phase or project, which stands a good chance of success. Indicates rewarding communication where old enmities are resolved, we move beyond the pain, heal wounds. In particular, those thorny situations where somebody gets hold of the wrong end of the stick and takes offence will often yield to the clarity this card brings in.

Bottom Line Interpretations (Tarantino): It's the right time to trust your instincts, take the initiative, and proceed. Be prepared to respond swiftly to any challenge or opportunity. There won't be time for studied reflection. Don't waste time beating around the bush. Say what you need to say. When you are ready to speak out, your words will be met with acceptance, understanding, and appreciation. Negative: at this point, no one understands what you think or where you stand. Unless you are more assertive, you will continue to miss the mark, ending up making only superficial changes and going nowhere fast. Underneath it all you know what you think and feel, but this gets obscured/lost in a sea of unnecessary words. Communicate clearly, softly, and deliberately.

Advice: Present your position with openness and emphasis. Overcome the tendency to hesitate. Call problems by their name. At the same time, beware of being swept away, applying too much force suddenly.

NINE OF WANDS: STRENGTH

TAROTNYMS

Inner strength put to practical purposes versus overcoming self-doubt/lack of focus

Strong contact with inner creative powers versus allowing negative thinking/self-doubt/past failures to hold one back

The courage/strength to face one's past and move forward/transform versus denying parts of our life and experience

ELEMENTAL SNAPSHOT

THE FLAMES OF HARMONY (INNER ENERGY)

MAIN SUMMARY MEANING:

Inner strength, power, health. Success after conflict. Tremendous force, recovery. Victory follows fear.

SYMBOLISM:

- Zodiac = Sagittarius (subtle energy, spiritual, swift, light, and elusive); Planet = Moon (inner, imagination, unconscious, reflective, illusive, emotion);
- The strong wand in the center connects with the moon and sun. Unconscious fears are made visible and we become stronger than we thought possible;

- The 10 flames and 8 downward pointing arrows indicate that energy is growing stronger, more so than any other wand card. Strive for balance and "live in the moment" in order to make the most of the energy available.

DIVINATION:

Latent powers are awakened and can be applied toward a purpose. Whatever our past, the 9 of Wands, Strength, reminds us that in being true to ourselves we release energies that will help us to deal with whatever we find within.

Your mistakes have special messages for you. To be able to admit you could have dealt with a situation better is, if you allow it to be, one of the most useful revelations of your life. Rather than feeling bad about your actions, allow yourself to consider what would have improved the outcome. Once you have done this, you'll store that away as new knowledge, and next time a similar situation occurs you'll remember, and act accordingly.

Bottom Line Interpretations (Tarantino): You've responded to difficulties with valor and are now in a superb position to reach your goals. Keep your sights on your goals while everything else changes. Your strength and power will continue to grow as you transcend day-to-day fluctuations. Follow a path of moderation and you are less likely to be thrown off balance. Negative: present circumstances have thrown you off balance. Now is the time to reconsider if you have adopted an extreme position. Stop getting thrown off course by reacting to every little thing that happens. Instead, remain flexible and stay neutral.

Advice: This card tells us to trust ourselves. We have everything we need. There is no necessity to analyze nor question. And absolutely no excuse to give in to doubt!

TEN OF WANDS: OPPRESSION

TAROTNYMS

Addressing the emotional contributions to our worries versus being oppressed by intense worries without recognizing our contribution

Struggling/working hard to be successful versus excessive stress from overwork and taking on too much responsibility

Giving up pleasing illusions and facing cold hard reality versus becoming bitter and cynical

Feelings of insecurity and lack of safety/wanting more versus taking pleasure and joy in the moment/ counting one's blessings

ELEMENTAL SNAPSHOT

THE FLAMES OF SELF-DETERMINATION (ENERGY FRUSTRATED)

MAIN SUMMARY MEANING:

Blocked or thwarted will. Oppression. Fire in its most destructive aspect. Cruelty, malice, selfishness, lying repression, ill will. Can also mean self-sacrifice and compassion.

SYMBOLISM:

- Zodiac = Sagittarius (subtle energy, spiritual, swift, light, and elusive); Planet = Saturn (slow, heavy, obstinate);

- The two "dorjes" represent bars, covering and enclosing the enormous energy behind. Great antipathy is suggested.

DIVINATION:

We want something badly, and yet we seem to stand no chance of getting it. We feel frustrated, irritable and disappointed.

Bottom Line Interpretations (Tarantino): Life is supplying you with an opportunity to stop being your own worst enemy. You're taking too much responsibility. In the name of everyday duty and obligation, you've lost track of your vision. What was once a pleasure has now become a burden. There's no time left for creativity, spontaneity, and freedom. Delegate. Ask for help. Negative: you are tired of feeling responsible for everything and everybody. If you want to revitalize your situation, start by taking better care of yourself. You need to relax and work at having fun. Let others pull their weight. Things will get done in due time without having to have your fingers in everything.

Advice: Consider whether this is a fleeting problem which will soon pass. If so, stop focusing on the negative and move on. If the frustration is more chronic, consider whether it is due to difficulties clearly communicating your feelings on a given topic, to somebody who has strong influence over our lives. Instead of presenting a bland and safe mask to the outside world, isolate the things that you really wish you could tell people around you who matter. Then consider why you might not be speaking your mind and what it will take to do so.

KNIGHT OF WANDS

TAROTNYMS

Idealistic/self-confidence versus intolerant

Active/forward moving/striving for better solutions/born entrepreneur/clever versus egotistic/petulant/brutal/cruel

Full of potential/creativity/good instincts/initiative/introducing new ways of looking at the world/self-determination versus poor team player/vain/self-absorbed/hard to treat others as equals

ELEMENTAL SNAPSHOT

THE FATHER OF THE CREATIVE IMAGINATION (DYNAMIC ENERGY)

MAIN SUMMARY MEANING:

The fiery part of fire. A man of activity, generosity, pride and swiftness. Uses his burning passion to clear the path as well as eliminate negativity, ignorance, and lethargy. If wrongly energized, it can mean cruelty, bigotry, petulance, brutal. Can burn himself out in the long run.

Dynamic forward motion, increased insight, coming changes. Mastery of growth and inner development.

SYMBOLISM:

- Zodiac = Sagittarius;
- Element = Fire;
- Flames of fire represent momentum, revolution, transformation, integrity, honesty;
- He sits on a leaping black horse symbolizing good instincts, activity, and courage;
- In his left hand, a burning torch symbolizing creative genius, focus, determination, burning away all negativity that stands in his way;
- His red cape is a king's mantle and is woven into the background, indicating the fire that emanates from within and is integrated into life;
- His helmet is ornamented with a unicorn's head symbolizes the third eye, insightfulness, perceptiveness, single minded focus, ability to see what is not seen by others;
- His armor is made of reptile skin, which symbolizes ability to transform himself in the moment, willingness to fight the good fight, coolly indifferent to distractions.

DIVINATION:

A card of happy news, and will be about, or delivered by a young man who is interested in sales and/or travel. Difficult situations will move in a constructive direction.

Bottom Line Interpretations (Tarantino): It's normal to be apprehensive when you're in the vortex of rapid change. Persevere. For the time being, trust your impulse to take charge. Be willing to make changes quickly. Be honest and straightforward in your communications and actions. Have faith in the bigger picture. Negative: A major revolution in your circumstances is at hand. You need to adapt to changes that are occurring. Nothing stays the same. The situation may not turn out as planned. Fate favors those who are adaptable. Even these hard times will pass and good fortune will follow.

Advice: Be apprehensive, yet cool, resolute and energetic; beware of untimely action, but willing to go forward with tense confidence in own ability.

QUEEN OF WANDS

Queen of Wands

TAROTNYMS

Energetic, powerful, passionate, assertive versus egotistical, inconsiderate jealous, and withholding

Mature, open-minded, strong willed, enterprising, confident versus manipulative, sensitive to criticism, denied recognition or admiration

Intuitive, mastery of emotions versus temperamental, bitchy

Demanding equality versus wanting submission

ELEMENTAL SNAPSHOT

THE MOTHER OF LOVE AND SEXUAL INSTINCTS

The watery part of fire. Adaptability, energy, calm authority, powers of attraction, compassion, generous but intolerant. If wrongly energized, stupid, obstinate, revengeful, domineering, vain, even snobbish, and quick to take offense.

SYMBOLISM:

- Zodiac = Aries;
- Element = Fire;
- Fiery flames represent transformation, primal spiritual energy;
- Her fiery crown symbolizes extreme perceptiveness;

- The queen sits on a fiery throne wearing an armor of scales with a fish emblem, symbolizing the union of water and fire, of intuitive recognition and emotional sensitivity and involvement;
- Eyes are closed in quiet ecstasy;
- The wand held in this fashion means to ground any realization in the earth as well as to allow others to share it;
- The pine cone at the end of the wand symbolizes transformation, spiritual growth;
- The leopard, on the head of which rests her hand, symbolizes her connection, acceptance, and mastery of her drives, passions and instincts.

DIVINATION:

Times are changing. If you acquire a complete understanding of the situation you are facing, you will know when to take the lead and when to assume a subordinate role.

Dealings with authority figures go well. Answers arrive when you talk things out with friends and lovers.

Bottom Line Interpretations (Tarantino): Intuitively, you know what to do. At the same time, you do not have to play "first fiddle" in this situation. Because you can see the far reaching potential of this situation, you can become impatient with any opposition. This will not help. Start by listening, and letting other people help you. Negative: when confronted with opposition, be less argumentative. Put aside your pride. Open your mind to new possibilities instead of closing down and becoming defensive.

Advice: Believe in yourself, don't be afraid to take the lead. Dare to dream but keep both feet firmly on the ground.

PRINCE OF WANDS

Prince of Wands

TAROTNYMS

Strong push/readiness for action/courage/bursting with creative energy versus impetuousness

Infectious hope in future possibilities/drive/new ideas versus lack of experience/follow through/prone to exaggeration

Enthusiasm/energetic/thirst for adventure versus impatient/risk-taking/uncertain outcome/capricious

Open versus naïve/fickle/breaking the rules/inadvertently destructive/impulsive/directionless

ELEMENTAL SNAPSHOT

THE SON OF WILLPOWER
(INEXPERIENCED ENERGY)

MAIN SUMMARY MEANING:

The airy part of fire. Intensity. Definiteness, openness, freedom. Youthful, passionate, daring, pioneering. Bravery, freedom, and adventure. Enormous capacity for love. Blossoming love, intuitive creativity, out of the darkness into the light. Noble and generous, given to defending strongly stated opinions that he may not hold himself but engages in merely for the sake of argument. When wrongly energized, proud, cruel, intolerant, cowardly, and prejudiced.

SYMBOLISM:

- Zodiac = Leo (pulling the card, symbol of creative energy);
- Element = Fire;
- Flames of fire symbolize passion, drive, ambition, enthusiasm, optimism;
- Seated in a chariot of fire and holding the phoenix wand, symbolizing the creative process and power and energy directed at the goal;
- Holding the reins loosely symbolizes trusting the process, following where passion leads perhaps more the directing it;
- His nakedness symbolizes that he is open and does not need to hide or protect himself;
- His rayed crown symbolizes strong will and intent, moving toward enlightenment;
- The dark behind the figure indicates the darkness he is leaving behind and a warning to be aware of external influences;
- The green of the flame indicates mastery of creative energy;
- The lotus leaf on his chest indicates a surrender to love, and along with the phoenix feathers, lifting him and allowing him to see the world from an elevated perspective;
- His legs form the number 4 (the number of the Emperor), indicating that he is a builder, creator of form;
- The yellow, red, and orange colors symbolize vitality, passion, and inspiration.

DIVINATION:

Nothing can hinder the creative flow. Moving beyond former limitations in thought.

Bottom Line Interpretations (Tarantino): Eager to accept the tests and challenges inherent in the goals you've set for yourself. Trust your sense of confidence and adventure and move full speed ahead. The road ahead is full of mysteries, intrigue, and new experiences. When challenges appear, use them to show just how much you can accomplish. You possess the courage, charisma, and stamina necessary to navigate any storm. Negative: you're stalled in stagnation and/or indecision. You seem to be having difficulty staying focused on your goals. Listening to others feeds rather than resolves your self-doubt. Think about what you really want to be doing.

Advice: You have all you need. Don't let yourself be slowed down or contained. Be careful of pride. Others judge you. Don't give into the temptation to scapegoat.

THE PRINCESS OF WANDS

TAROTNYMS

Coming into one's own/carefree/outgoing/passionate/free versus careless/remaining inwardly vulnerable and insecure

Discovering/exploring/accepting one's power/sexuality versus ambivalence/lack of commitment

Willingness for union/able to provoke passionate entanglement versus teasing/titillation/theatrical/shallow/faithless

Spontaneous/independent versus irresponsible/sending the wrong signal/recognition for recognition's sake/vanity

ELEMENTAL SNAPSHOT

THE DAUGHTER OF FIRE
(PASSIONATE ENERGY)

MAIN SUMMARY MEANING:

The earthly aspect of fire, bring freed from fear, new beginning, optimism, brilliant and daring, expressive and enthusiastic, increased perception. Coming into one's own, discovering and accepting one's power and sexuality. When wrongly energized can be superficial, theatrical, shallow, cruel, unreliable, and faithless.

SYMBOLISM:

- Element = Fire;

- Naked, open, unprotected, has the Tiger "by the tail," symbolizing that despite being afraid, she takes hold of her fears and inner demons and continues;

- She dances on a huge flame, a river of fire symbolizing energy, instinctual drive, and ambition;

- The altar is decorated with ram's heads, the fire of spring, new beginnings. The roses symbolize the changes she has gone through and sacrifices made;

- The wand with solar disk symbolizes the passion that empowers us, moves us to action;

- The fiery red background symbolizes, warmth, passion, vitality, and flaming energy;

- The horns/antennae extended from the head symbolize perceptiveness/youthful, exaggerated sense of justice and ethics.

DIVINATION:

There will be confidence, decisive action, and an assertive leap forward into the heart of your life. It can indicate a spiritual breakthrough, which will always include the courage to face your fears, and see them for what they truly are.

Independent, usually outspoken (even a touch stubborn), people who are unafraid to express her needs/desires or anger. Their engagement with life is total. They don't waste time on negative pursuits and often end up learning lessons the hard way.

Bottom Line Interpretations (Tarantino): There's no such thing as a "sure thing." Move forward despite your anxieties. You're empowered to act with inspiration and vitality. Trust your insights and don't be afraid to exert a little pressure and question authority. Your situation is unique and calls for innovative ideas and inspirations. Negative: you are going to have to work a lot hard than you thought. Your present state of mind is unproductive. It's time to abandon the false comfort of retreat and procrastination. Focusing on the risks rather than reaching your heart's desire has sapped your energy. "Take the tiger by the tail," and get on with things.

Advice: Everyone wants to get things done quickly. Don't overlook important details in the rush to completion.

 CUPS:

The element of water, standing for inner emotion or reality, love, feeling, relationship (world of Briah).

The element of Water embodies the primeval emotion and intuition; it is passivity and placidity, receptivity and responsiveness. Water is fluid, adaptive and pragmatic; it will always go the way of the least resistance, changing its course at the slightest disturbance. With no outer influence, water won't move.

Water is associated with the level Neshamah and the world of Briah, the dark unconscious receiving the spark of life from the Fire thus giving birth to creation. But, the creation born in the Water is not a creation that actually creates anything - that act will be left to Air (Yetzirah) and Earth (Assiah).

When looking at the qualities of the elements, we remember that Water is considered as cold. Warm power separates and dissolves, while the cold power unites and binds, which Water does without ever taking a defined form. It will mix and solve, dissolve and rearrange, change and transform. Water is the Mother who receives the semen and nurtures the embryo but leaves the actual birth to someone else.

The element of Water as the realm of emotion, subconscious and intuition is often seen in an over-romanticized manner. What people tend to forget is that conscious 'emotion', in the very moment we are aware of one, is but our mind's transcription of the original emotion. Subconscious does not need telling - in the moment we are aware of it, it is not 'sub' anymore - it is conscious. And what often gets identified as 'intuition' is usually the first conclusion the mind had jumped on. A thought, not a feeling. And the very moment we have it in our 'thoughts' it is Yetzirah at work, not Briah.

The world of Briah is a dark and cold world, a bottomless pit of archaic, unsorted notions, a quicksand of quicksilver and yet in slow motion, if any motion at all. Quiet, limitless, passive, a black hole into some unknown dimension. Yet, Water is also a life-giver, as much as no life would be possible on this planet without water, the spiritual being would be nowhere without Water as well.

In the Tarot Water is associated with the Suit of Cups.

ACE OF CUPS

TAROTNYMS

Blissfulness/happiness/heart's desire versus irrational/blind love/longing for love

A journey to the heart/emergence of true love/falling in love (altruism/trust/faith)/a beginning (project/life) versus not seeing the complete picture/caught up in the moment

Receptivity/connection versus seeking deeper joy/meaning in life

Giving versus loss of self/emotionally starving

ELEMENTAL SNAPSHOT

THE SOURCE OF EMOTION (PURE FEELING)

MAIN SUMMARY MEANING:

Fertility, productivity, pleasure, happiness, beauty, aimless love. This is a card which is connected to our most precious and heartfelt desires. It indicates the things that we hold most dear, our deepest and most intimate feelings and needs.

SYMBOLISM:

Holy Grail, or in pagan terms, the Cauldron of Kerridwyn, source of loving openness, inspiration and granter of wishes and dreams. The beam of light unites Earth and Cosmos. The cup is the medium for bringing together upper and lower, inner and outer, spirit with emotion. The waters of understanding pour through the cup symbolizing sensitivity and receptiveness in its purest form. White lotus is a symbol of love of a giving nature. The cup is fed from within. The two blue-green serpents on the handles symbolize renewal of the soul. The brown colored waves are a reminder that the energy of emotion can be experienced right here on earth.

DIVINATION:

Represents the beginning of love, fertility and creativity. It is a card to inspire confidence and happiness. When it turns up a reading of an everyday nature it can indicate the start of a loving relationship (of either the romantic or friendship variety); it can represent the beginning of a project in which a great deal of loving energy is invested; or sometimes it can reveal conception –the beginning of a new life.

Bottom Line Interpretations (Tarantino): Take the opportunity to express exactly how you feel. Don't waste energy trying to analyze why everything seems to be working. Instead, open your heart. Follow your passions, trust your instincts. To reach your goals, you must continue to take risks, be innovative, and have confidence in your convictions. There's never been a better time to promote yourself, your ideas, or your situation. Negative: Inability to connect with your emotions has left you isolated. The very core of your being feels unloved and unlovable. How you feel influences your actions. Accept yourself as you are right now. Make a list of the things in your life that are positive and productive.

Advice: If you are looking at the Ace of Cups indicating a new relationship, then there will also be people cards up. If it is a romantic relationship, expect to see other good Cups, and perhaps the Lovers. Friendship will be more indicated by Wand type good cards. Pregnancy will usually come up with other cards which also indicate pregnancy Princess of Disks, Ace of Wands, and possibly the Empress.

The beginning of a project will normally have something like the Star or the Priestess, and Disks around it. These will help you to determine the viability of the project.

When this card comes up with the Hierophant, Sun, Moon or sometimes with Death, we must see ourselves as entering into a major transformational period.

TWO OF CUPS: LOVE

TAROTNYMS

Development of a relationship consistent with one's desires/wishes versus identifying one's desires and wishes in order to be prepared to enter into a relationship

An important, positive encounter characterized by harmony, trust, cooperation, good working climate versus being on the lookout/being certain it's real/questions about whether its real

Deep emotional exchange versus wishing a superficial relationship might deepen, go further/conflict of interests

Reconciliation/renewal of relationship versus desire for reconciliation/renewal of a relationship that has caused paint/disappointment

ELEMENTAL SNAPSHOT

THE WATER OF ATTRACTION (EMOTIONAL CONNECTION)

MAIN SUMMARY MEANING:

Love, cooperation, trust, harmony, radiant joy/ecstasy, pleasure, warm friendship. Happy relationships, emotional exchange. A deep, emotional exchange possible, reconciliation.

SYMBOLISM:

- Zodiac = Cancer (receptive sign); Planet = Venus (sign of love);

- Two cups overflowing on a calm sea, filled by a large pink lotus (symbol of love of a giving kind). Dolphins characterize the exchange of feelings. The background is divided into three colors: (1) blue for emotion; (2) yellow-green for deep joy (yellow); and (3) green, the energy of renewal and healing.

DIVINATION:

Meaningful relationship in your life will strengthen and grow, developing into exactly what you need it to be, or, it might point up a new relationship which has recently begun and which will grow into a deep and lasting friendship or affair.

If it relates to the inner journey, then it tells you to put your attention in the moment, to leave the past behind, and to let yourself be free to enjoy everything that comes your way. If it relates to outer events, it may point to a forthcoming reconciliation in a relationship where there has been pain and disappointment–this need not be a love affair, it can cover many different types of loving relationship.

Bottom Line Interpretations (Tarantino): If you are not already involved in a mutually supportive relationship, you can expect to be very soon. Any partnership created on this level is destined for success. Negative: You have a heartfelt desire to interact/connect with others. Be receptive to the situation at hand. Misunderstanding can easily occur if you shut yourself off. If you are open, what you need will come to you. Begin by becoming the person you want to attract. Acknowledge your own needs and desires.

Advice: Pay attention to the love coming to you now. Remain open, and let it enter you and go deep inside.

THREE OF CUPS: ABUNDANCE

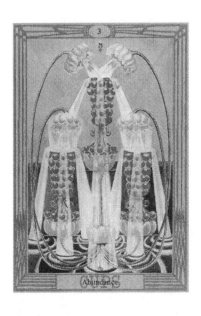

TAROTNYMS

Joy and fulfilment in the emotional/relational realm versus devoting one's self completely to a loving/committed partnership

Opening one's self to life in complete abundance versus being fearful of being hurt/knowing that nothing lasts forever/feeling selfish

What one wants to achieve is now within sight/reach versus needing to reach out/take a risk (chance)

Return to health/well-being versus enjoying the pleasures/relationships available despite current struggles

ELEMENTAL SNAPSHOT

THE WATER OF CONCEPTION (EMOTIONAL ABUNDANCE)

MAIN SUMMARY MEANING:

Abundance, spiritual fertility, plenty, hospitality, pleasure, sensuality, love kindness, bounty, success.

SYMBOLISM:

- Zodiac = Cancer (the most receptive sign); Planet = Mercury (will and swiftness). In other words, will finds receptivity;

- Pomegranates, a rare and delicious fruit, symbolize the vital treasures in uncommon love, shared only by a small circle of people. Their abundance in this card carries a warning: emotional pleasure can be seductive and addictive, thereby resisting transformation and growth. Three cups may symbolize three important people with whom a person shares great intimacy.

DIVINATION:

If a person has been unwell, it calls for a return to health.

Bottom Line Interpretations (Tarantino): You are entering a very happy period in your life. Delight in the camaraderie, success, and good feelings. There is optimism in the air. Let others know how strongly you feel. To reach your goals, seek out like-minded people (same interests and vision), and network. Abundance and prosperity will flow into your life in direct proportion to how willing you are to ask for what you need. Negative: Give up trying to do this alone. Seek out and accept help. Overcome any fear of rejection. Take an emotional risk. Develop a support system and express your feelings openly. Celebrate life in everything you do.

Advice: Intimate relationships are rare, care for them with respect and gratitude.

May indicate that the good things in life, while to be enjoyed, are not necessarily to be trusted.

FOUR OF CUPS: LUXURY

TAROTNYMS

Strong/stable, predictable relationships/emotional life versus the familiar is boring, predictable, stale, empty/taking stable relationships or granted

Peace, amity, tranquility versus dull, lacking adventure, more show than real, working hard at not losing what one has rather than truly living

Deeply loved, in good health, tranquility versus forgetting what it is like not be lonely/being careless about the way we treat those who love us/ always wanting more

THE WATER OF DEVELOPED FEMININITY (EMOTIONAL ORDER)

Luxury. Abandonment to desire. Weakness, injustice, pleasure mixed with anxiety, decay in the fruits of pleasure. Dissatisfaction, boredom. Oppression by the familiar.

SYMBOLISM:

- Zodiac = Cancer (the most receptive); Planet = Moon (inner, imagination, unconscious, reflective, illusive, emotion)

- The fours, in numerological terms, relate to the four card of the major arcana, the Emperor. Fours are all about stability, foundation, and order. Cups are related to relationships and emotions. Four of cups therefore implies stability in a relationship, or emotional stability.

- The four cups stand for the wealth of feelings at hand whose roots are deep but they rest on a sea that is no longer still. The pink lotus from which feelings flow is looking a little worse for the wear and has a multiple stem, symbolizing that energy has lost its original purity. The water flows in the shape of pointed arrow into the second set of cup, indicating a loss of original form and fluidity. The sky has darkened, warning of a potential storm where the familiar becomes oppressive.

DIVINATION:

Four of cups is actually an auspicious card that indicates a strong marriage, steady friendship or a stable home life. To the more adventurous, such ideas might seem a bit dull. If the four of cups greets you, you probably won't win the lottery, but your life may be blessed with peace, amity and tranquility.

A card with "a sting in its tail." Sometimes, when we are loved deeply and for a long period of time, we are foolish enough to forget what it feels like when we are lonely and unloved. We begin to get careless about the ways in which we treat those people who love us. We may hanker after love from someone outside our circle, instead of valuing those people closer to hand who love us from the bottom of their hearts.

In other words, we can begin to take love for granted. And there are three things in this world we are all silly to take for granted—love, good health and tranquility. Every one of them slips away silently if we stop paying it due attention.

With great riches (emotionally, spiritually, or otherwise), it is easy to become restless, even bored, to spend time thinking about what might have been or what one is missing out on.

An emphasis on what the individual wants or desires supplants what the whole body wishes, thereby creating instability.

Bottom Line Interpretations (Tarantino): Stop and examine where your feelings are taking you. Being self-absorbed and self-centered has caused you to be oblivious to everything going on around you. Things may look right on the surface, but you are headed for trouble unless you attend to events around you. Don't let emotions overpower your rational mind. Work at bringing balance (emotional) back in your life and something new will be offered. Focus on the long run rather than acting on momentary feelings. Negative: buried feelings leave you feeling cold and aloof. Give voice to the feelings and you release vital energy and things will start moving again.

Advice: Danger exists when our riches take on a life of their own, moderation is lost, and we become driven by emotions unconsciously.

It's a reminder of the need for honor and duty to be maintained in your relationship. You may be tempted by someone or something that would draw you away from your current stable situation.

FIVE OF CUPS: DISAPPOINTMENT

A period of emotional change/disruption/turbulence (betrayal, sadness, misfortune) versus all changes are temporary/staying focused on what lies ahead rather than what is lost

Lack of sense of control/security/dominance of circumstances over desires versus time to consider our expectations/return to basics

Imbalance in emotional expression/control of appetites (desires) versus becoming more reflective/seeking other emotional outlets/attending to our relationships

Destructive energy smoldering beneath the surface but ignored versus facing issues directly makes transformation possible

ELEMENTAL SNAPSHOT

THE WATER OF STAGNATION (EMOTIONAL DISAPPOINTMENTS)

MAIN SUMMARY MEANING:

Disappointment, unexpected disturbance, misfortune, heartache, lack of kindness from friends, betrayal, resentment, sadness, regret.

SYMBOLISM:

- Zodiac = Scorpio (dark, all-consuming nature); Planet = Mars (aggression and power);

- The 5 of Cups merges the instability of the 5's with the element of Water. As Water is representative of emotions, in the 5 of Cups, our feelings are subjected to great (and oftentimes uncontrollable) turbulence. It is important to remember that all 5's deal with change – a metaphorical death of sorts – in varying degrees. In the 5 of Cups, this change is experienced as loss;

- The cups are empty and arranged in an inverted pentacle symbolizing the triumph of matter over spirit (circumstances over will/desire). The lotus (symbol of love) leaves are dry and torn by the hot wind. Although they reach toward each other, they do not touch, symbolizing a loss of connection. The murky green sea is arid and stagnant symbolizing that the destructive energy now dominating the scene has been smoldering beneath the surface for some time but were ignored;

- The orange-red sky in the background symbolizes anger, frustration and the loss of faith and courage. Our sense of security and control has been disrupted. When we experience loss, one of the first things to crumble is our faith in a "just world." In the face of loss, many of us find ourselves resorting to unhealthy habits that serve as temporary Band-Aids for our pain;

- The roots of the lotus are curled in the shape of a butterfly symbolizing the possibility of transformation.

DIVINATION:

Anticipated pleasure has been or is on the verge of being frustrated.

Bottom Line Interpretations (Tarantino): You've lost something you cared deeply about. If you were heavily invested in one particular outcome, its failure can be devastating. You're angry with yourself for not seeing this coming. Consider whether your expectations were realistic and whether you were over emotionally invested. Remember that something new always grows from the ashes of the old. Negative: disappointment, disillusionment, and grief about a situation/relationship in which you were emotionally invested. You let unfounded expectations and wishful thinking cloud your judgment. With this failure, comes wisdom. That said, you are well on your way to picking up the pieces and turning your life around. Be willing to keep dreaming.

Advice: The direction the wind takes at any one time is temporary. It's easy to stay fixed on what has been lost, rather than what remains and lies ahead.

When this card comes up, it's worth taking a good look at ones expectations. Are they unrealistic?

It can also warn about an old difficulty, or that—realistic or not—our expectations are about to be disappointed. Often this will happen in an emotional situation (because this is a Cup card) but can happen elsewhere in our lives too, because disappointment itself is an emotion and therefore belongs to Cups. Aside from locating where the problem lies, there's rarely much that can be done except preparing ourselves to accept the inevitable consequence of being alive (into each life a little rain must fall).

SIX OF CUPS: PLEASURE

TAROTNYMS

Richness of feeling, well-being, and close emotional ties without effort or strain versus readiness to dive in but need to make changes to make pleasure possible

Joyful creation, vitality, happiness, health, and success versus fear of disappointment/caught in prior hurts/guilty conscious/selfishness

Pleasure versus debauchery/unsatisfied/forgetting other's needs

ELEMENTAL SNAPSHOT

THE WATER OF THE JOY OF LIFE AND INNER HARMONY (EMOTIONAL PEACE)

MAIN SUMMARY MEANING:

Pleasure, well-being, harmony of natural forces without effort or strain. Ease, satisfaction, happiness, success. Fulfillment of sexual will. Beginning of a steady increase, fertility. It's important to recognize, with this card, that its influence extends only to established relationships—those which already have a history of their own. It will come up in a reading to indicate major steps forward, strengthened commitment, marriage, recovery after trial.

SYMBOLISM:

- Zodiac = Scorpio (all consuming); Planet = Sun (pure energy);
- As a six card, there is balance and harmony present. The lotus stems

are glowing symbolizing vitality, indicating readiness for pleasurable interaction with the beloved. The stems are made of copper (a healing element) and grouped in an elaborate movement (butterfly), water gushes into them, they are full but not overflowing. Copper cups, the symbol of internal healing. Snakes coiled in each cup symbolizing the transformational power of sex when it is experienced naturally.

DIVINATION:

The fear of disappointment has been overcome (5 of cups). Readiness to dive in, let go. Existing relationships broaden and deepen, giving an extended sense of contentment and satisfaction. We are comfortable with our feelings and are enjoying the pleasures of life.

Bottom Line Interpretations (Tarantino): Life is unfolding according to plan. Things are happening quickly so be sure to enjoy each step of the process. The future is not promised to you, only now. So, take time to notice the pleasures of everyday life. Negative: it can be difficult to enjoy the simple pleasures of life. It's no surprise you are feeling like life is passing you by. Consider making a list of things you like to do just for fun and doing one each day.

Advice: An invitation to give yourself up to the richness of your emotions. Make a point of taking the time to give yourself up to pleasure, however you define it. Warns of vanity, presumptuousness, thanklessness. Don't let the past distract from the present.

SEVEN OF CUPS: DEBAUCH

TAROTNYMS

Deep longing for connection/happiness/bliss versus seeking experiences/engaging in behaviors that bring only transitory joy/infantile dependence/giving in to temptation

Surrounded by pleasures versus unable to choose and losing all/greedily taking all/giving in to temptations or transitory, empty pleasures

Seeking transcendental/consciousness-raising experiences/chasing bliss versus evasion of real life/false hopes/uncritical seductibility/building castles in the air

Need to see things as they are/lower expectations/limit self to what is feasible versus caught in poisonous atmosphere/deceptive feelings/relationships

ELEMENTAL SNAPSHOT

THE WATER OF DELUSION
(EMOTIONAL INDULGENCE)

MAIN SUMMARY MEANING:

Delusion, illusory success, addiction, intoxication, guilt, deceit, promises unfulfilled, lust, dissipation of love and friendship. The card is a reminder of the fatal ease with which a sacrament can be profaned and prostituted. Lose touch with the highest, and the holiest mysteries of nature become obscene and shameful secrets of a guilty conscience.

SYMBOLISM:

- Zodiac = Scorpio (all consuming); Planet = Venus (sign of love);

- Everything looks stagnant and decaying. The lotuses have become poisonous, dropping green slime into blue cups. They are arranged in two descending triangles, the lowest cup much larger than the rest (symbolizing external splendor but internal corruption) has sunk beneath the surface (symbolizing drowning in feelings). There has been too much of a good thing, and overindulgence has taken its toll.

DIVINATION:

Without fail, when this card appears we must expect to be subjected to some kind of temptation or test. We must be on our guard for making the exact mistake that it tells us is possible. Temptations come in many shapes and forms, some of these are minor, and others much more serious. The 7 of Cups deals primarily with sensual pleasures (sex, food, money, status).

Sometimes, the card indicates that we are surrounded by a multitude of different pleasures, and cannot quite make our minds up which ones to choose, out of the many available to us. In so doing, we miss the boat altogether and end up with nothing. Or, alternatively, we greedily snatch at everything we see, possibly missing the real treasure that is waiting for us to notice it.

Emotions are out of balance, a deep disappointment has not been resolved. Trying to cover wounds with diversions is not working. After every binge or flight, the problem remains.

Bottom Line Interpretations (Tarantino): Examine your options carefully before committing. At the moment, you are drowning in emotions. Your current state can color your sense of reason and negatively affect decisions. Sometimes we can move so deeply into our emotions that we get bogged down and need professional help to find out way out. Take a look at the practical solutions available to you. Negative: your feelings are much deeper than they may appear on the surface. Put your critical judgment aside and begin expressing your emotions. The time has come to put reason aside, and follow your heart.

Advice: It's time to open one's eyes and face reality, stop avoiding the problem as this increases stagnation of emotional energy.

Greed, triviality, surrender of moral ethics are the big problems when this card appears. We must guard firmly against any of these things, holding hard to our sense of love and goodness.

We will always be tempted to do things that we will later regret, and we will find ourselves weak-willed when it comes to choosing what we know is the right course of action.

EIGHT OF CUPS: INDOLENCE

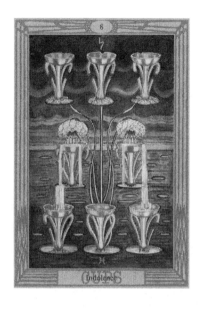

TAROTNYMS

Know there are challenging issues/need to change/move on/renewal (spiritually/morally/relationally) versus too tired/absence of passion/feeling/loss of interest/lack of motivation

Time to find a purpose/meaning/connection/time to target one issue/relationship versus resignation/giving up/lack of effort/self-pity

Self-sacrifice/leaving behind material pursuits for a higher purpose versus spiritually empty perhaps corrupt (words only)/running on empty

ELEMENTAL SNAPSHOT

THE WATERS OF RESIGNATION (EMOTIONAL APATHY)

MAIN SUMMARY MEANING:

Indolence (after debauchery), abandoned or temporary success, declining interest, instability, misery, transience.

SYMBOLISM:

- Zodiac = Pisces (sign of personality and soul/peace and the spiritual); Planet = Saturn (slow, heavy, obstinate);
- The energy has fizzled, the handles of the copper cups are broken, symbolizing too much pleasure and indulgence, as well as it being "hard to get a handle" on matters. The water of emotion stands, and is not

replenished by a spring. The two remaining lotus flowers continue to spill out their energies but to no effect as the stagnant water swallows up its freshness and vitality.

DIVINATION:

Energy is stagnating now; there is no renewal, no cleansing flow. Instead, there is apathy and disappointment. If this state of affairs is allowed to continue, it will reflect negatively into daily life, causing disturbance in the domestic and material situation.

May mean leaving material success for something higher. Upheaval, walking away from a relationship.

Bottom Line Interpretations (Tarantino): Take better care of yourself by setting limits on your time, energy, and resources. You have a vague feeling that something is missing. Consider the possibility that you have spent more time on others than yourself. Negative: Balance and vitality are about to returning. Remember, self-nurturing and setting boundaries are important. Say yes when you mean yes and no when no is what you mean.

Advice: A nasty and potentially dangerous situation which must be addressed if it is to be cleared out of the way. You may, though, feel tired and apathetic about challenging issues which seem too big or too stubborn to deal with.

If you are currently feeling quite trapped by life, then today is a day where you can take steps to change circumstance affecting you. Target one area which is taking more energy from you than it gives back. Think through your reactions and responses to this situation. Consider whether you're tending to slide a bit toward feeling like a victim—don't judge this, just consider it. If you judge something that sensitive, you will become defensive, and therefore be unable to tackle the problem properly.

You've wasted enough energy on people who give no return. You feel empty and dry, after having tried. The more energy poured into this relationship, the more in a rut things end up.

NINE OF CUPS: HAPPINESS

TAROTNYMS

Stable, balanced, abundant emotional/spiritual/relational life versus complacency/caught up in effusive feelings/displays

Happiness, contentment, joy, feeling blessed versus forgetting to count one's blessings/being aware/thankful for what one has

Period of high achievement resulting in a sense of pleasure/satisfaction versus vanity and conceit/lack of generosity/awareness of the needs of others

ELEMENTAL SNAPSHOT

THE WATER OF HAPPINESS
(EMOTIONAL WELL-BEING)

MAIN SUMMARY MEANING:

Happiness, complete success, pleasure, physical well-being. Could lead to vanity, conceit, and overindulgence.

SYMBOLISM:

- Zodiac = Pisces (sign of personality and soul/peace and the spiritual); Planet = Jupiter (luck and expansion):
- The nine cups are arranged in a square, and are filled and overflowing with water, symbolizing a stable, balanced, and abundant emotional life, deeply rooted joy and sense of blessedness.

DIVINATION:

A sense of inner fulfilment and bliss, which radiates outward to touch everybody with whom you come into contact. At a spiritual level, we're talking about inner harmony, contentment and tranquility—an appreciation of the High Powers, feeling at one with the Universe. This feeling leads to feeling that we are blessed by life.

On an everyday level, the card will often come up to mark periods of high achievement, and the resulting sense of pleasure and satisfaction. It will also come up to acknowledge joy and happiness in an emotional relationship.

Bottom Line Interpretations (Tarantino): Satisfaction, happiness and contentment are about to surface in your life. A long cherished dream becomes a reality. You've earned this period of peace and goodwill. Celebrate your good fortune and hard work. Be generous and compassionate toward others. Openly expressing your feelings will attract more opportunities. Negative: now is full of possibilities even if you can't see them. To benefit, you must cooperate by eliminating pessimism. An illusion of hopelessness may be detracting from your success and happiness. Do something that puts a smile on your face.

Advice: In the hurly burly of modern life it's easy to forget to count our blessings. And in so doing, we lose sight of a very basic spiritual truth—love is all around us. Beauty springs up in the most unexpected places. Radiance and wonder abound in this world of ours.

TEN OF CUPS: SATIETY

TAROTNYMS

Emotional/spiritual/relational harmony/fulfillment versus searching for fulfillment in these areas/inner emptiness/ recognition that there is no more that can be experienced/obtained/gained

A blissful moment full of contentment versus nothing lasts forever/bittersweet/all things must pass/no further increase in intensity/prepare one's self for a coming change by slowly opening up to new tasks/experiences

The end of a cycle of life/development versus stagnation/denial

ELEMENTAL SNAPSHOT

THE WATER OF COMPLETENESS (EMOTIONAL FULFILLMENT)

MAIN SUMMARY MEANING:

Contentment, deep fulfillment, pursuit of pleasure crowned with perfect success but incomplete, matters arranged and desired outcome as wished, lasting success, peacemaking, generosity. Risk of waste, dissipation, overindulgence, pity, stagnation.

SYMBOLISM:

- Zodiac = Pisces (sign of personality and soul/peace and the spiritual); Planet = Mars (aggression and power);

- The ten cups are arranged in the 'Tree of Life,' indicating everything is in its right place and in harmonious order. The oversized lotus at the top is an indication of the wealth of love received which overflows and pours into all who take part. The handles of the cups are made of rams' horns, and made of gold, indicating complete transformation. The fragile being has the decisiveness needed to bring forth into the outer world the beauty which it holds deep within. At the same time, the cups are unstable, because of the influence of Mars (representing the disruptive force which attacks any perfection) in Pisces (representing peace and the spiritual). This is as happy as a person dares get.

DIVINATION:

A sanctuary card. All relationships will continue to grow and develop. It indicates a blissful moment in time where we feel contented, happy and emotionally satisfied. It's easy to be at one with the Universe when you feel this blessed.

Bottom Line Interpretations (Tarantino): Success is inevitable. Commit to move past satiety to rebirth and further growth. Direct your passion and sense of fulfillment toward building the foundation for your next venture. Negative: time to let go and move on. Don't cling to old accomplishments. Don't let comfort could your passion. Get back into the game.

Advice: Unfortunately there's a word of warning: it won't last forever. Therefore, engage deeply with the energies around you. Don't take them for granted, nor look for problems. Just make sure you enjoy what's happening, and allow your sense of fulfilment to radiate from you.

KNIGHT OF CUPS

TAROTNYMS

Creative/visionary/charismatic versus impractical/unreliable/lacking follow through/needing to find outlet for artistic/social/helpful side

Sensitive/romantic/intense/charming versus a silver tongue/unfaithful

Open and caring/sympathetic versus insecure/needing reassurance/selfish/needing to set boundaries so as not to be taken advantage of for one's kindness

Balance between idealistic striving and instinctive urges versus lack of balance/disappointment and misunderstanding when the world and people do not live up to hopes/dreams

ELEMENTAL SNAPSHOT

THE FATHER OF SYMPATHY
(EMOTIONAL OPENNESS)

MAIN SUMMARY MEANING:

The fiery part of water. A man who is a graceful dilettante, amiable in a passive way, quick to respond to attraction and easily enthusiastic, exceedingly sensitive but little depth of character. He acts spontaneously and communicates from his heart. Since he lives in the moment, he is always moving on to the next hunch or feeling. Can also indicate a sensual and idle man, prone to melancholy or drug abuse.

SYMBOLISM:

- Zodiac = Pisces;
- Element = Water;
- A bareheaded warrior indicating openness, trusting, and vulnerable, freewheeling intellect and sureness;
- In green armor symbolizing communication of feelings, intuition, and imagination;
- White wings, flying high on imagination, intuition, and emotions;
- On a white horse, indicating a willingness to take action and purity of expression;
- In his hand, he holds a cup/grail, from which a crab emerges, the cardinal sign of water indicating inner absorption;
- The peacock symbolizes the brilliance of water (emotion), dramatic execution, ego, flamboyance;
- Blue symbolizes emotional wisdom; green, creative expression; red/orange, energy, intensity, vitality.

DIVINATION:

This card represents a contradiction. Most often when it appears, it will indicate an actual person who has influence. However sometimes it can also indicate a mood shift or a change of mode.

Since the Suit of Cups is all about love and loving relationships, it's easy to see how the Knight can be regarded as the lover of the cards. When representing a mood shift, the card can indicate the period where a man falls in love. When it represents a person he will be a complex and highly emotional being—creative and visionary, sensitive (and sometimes over-sensitive), romantic and intense. He will give the impression of being open and caring, though this is often misleading; the Knight of Cups is often subject to intense insecurity, needing constant re-assurance and attention.

He is attracted and attractive to women, and enjoys basking in their company. He will often be very charming, with a silver tongue and a powerful personal agenda. He will rarely manage practical matters well, tending to place rather more importance on buying two dozen red roses, than paying the bills. At his worst, he can be inconstant, unfaithful and selfish. The mixture of fire and water indicate a tendency to mismanage affairs, and may have a string of failures and disasters.

Bottom Line Interpretations (Tarantino): Listen to your intuition. Trust, communicate, and act on your feelings. Negative: you are having a problem expressing yourself. You won't get anywhere pretending you don't feel as you do. You may think you are protecting yourself, but you are actually suppressing the very energy you need to succeed. Let yourself be vulnerable in expressing your needs and desires. False pride will only prevent you from getting what you want.

Advice: On a day when this card comes up, it might be useful to have a think about the ways in which energy flows through your life and home.

QUEEN OF CUPS

TAROTNYMS

Reflective/empathic/sensitive/devotion versus absorbing the energy/opinions of context/easily influenced/lack of identity

Kind/gentle/tranquil versus passive/dependent/unable to stand on one's own

Psychic/intuitive/healing/mystical versus untouchable/mysterious/unclear/confusing

Desire to merge versus disappearing/losing one's self

ELEMENTAL SNAPSHOT

THE MOTHER OF THE SOURCE
(EMOTIONAL ATTUNEMENT)

MAIN SUMMARY MEANING:

The watery part of water. An observer, dreamy, illusive, tranquil, poetic, imaginative, kind yet passive. Having a reflective nature and neutral stance. This card (and the person) is very susceptible to other cards (people) influences.

SYMBOLISM:

- Zodiac = Cancer (sign of receptivity);
- Planet = Neptune (sign of intuition, understanding, emotion);
- Enthroned on water, meaning intuition, ability to mirror, empathize;
- The watery veil is a symbol for mystery and illusion. You cannot see the form

unless you look closely. The card symbolizes dreaminess, illusion, tranquility;

- Still water indicates a reflective nature. To see the Truth of her is nearly impossible as she reflects the nature of the observer in great perfection. She transmits everything. Her foremost ability in this area is a talent for simply absorbing energies around her and reflecting them back, unchanged;
- Lotus in the right hand stands for love. Also, symbol of spring, harbinger of the new;
- There are two water lilies indicative of balance and neutrality;
- The stork is a symbol for nurturing and compassion;
- The color blue indicates emotional wisdom and intelligence; yellow-gold, spirit; green, creativity.

DIVINATION:

She can often be a revealer for those around her. On the other hand, if gentleness and tranquility convert to weakness and unspoken resentment, she may nurture for the sake of inducing dependency, and places undue importance on being in a relationship, no matter what its quality. She will believe herself unable to stand alone.

Her reflective quality backfires so that she begins to take on the attitudes and thoughts of others. When this happens she begins to show signs of feeling victimized.

Bottom Line Interpretations (Tarantino): The forces affecting you may be elusive and fluid, so don't rely on outside circumstances to guide you. Your intuition is critical to your success. Listen with a quiet mind and open heart, looking for signals that tell you when to move and when to stay still. Negative: this is a time for practical, no-nonsense behavior. Do your homework before proceeding. At the moment, the difficulty is more about your conflicted internal state rather than the external state of affairs.

Advice: A time to reflect about love, and to seek out beauty. But since this card is an inward looking one, in many respects, we need to look at ourselves more than we look outside.

PRINCE OF CUPS

TAROTNYMS

Combining the depth of feeling with the heights of perception versus intellectual flights of fancy/inability to express our feelings or do more than express our feelings/hopes

Driven by a quest for transformation/higher plane or power/deep reaching character development/self-sacrifice versus seeking recognition

Idealistic/protective/romantic versus naïve/seductive/boundless fantasy/unfaithful/phony

ELEMENTAL SNAPSHOT

THE SON OF TRANSFORMATION (EMOTIONAL IDEALISM)

MAIN SUMMARY MEANING:

The Airy part of water. Subtle, secret, craft, ruthless, ambition. Calm on the outside, intensely passionate, even violent on the inside. Caring intensely for power, can be without conscience, and therefore not trusted by others.

SYMBOLISM:

- Zodiac = Scorpio (all consuming);
- Element = water;
- Air, in the context of water, symbolizes strong passions, as does the astrological sign Scorpio;

- The prince is naked symbolizing that he trusts his feelings, but is detached from his thoughts;

- The prince's coach, resembles a seashell, and is drawn by a scorpion/eagle, hinting at the possibility of transformation. The coach drives over emotions (water) but never touches it indicating a preference for keeping deeper emotions hidden;

- The eagle on the helmet of the prince indicates being driven by powerful emotions;

- The lotus is turned downward until he learns to integrate and manage the emotions. Similarly, his wings are made of gas;

- From the cup a snake arises captivating the driver's attention, symbolizing his focus on transformation;

- The color blue symbolizes emotional intelligence;
green, creativity.

DIVINATION:

Emotionally they can sometimes be turbulent and moody, but can also often hide their emotions and refuse to share them with others. However, having a highly developed sensitivity to emotional ups and downs, they will identify yours even before you have. Talking to somebody like this about emotional matters is usually a rewarding experience, because they are highly perceptive and use their intuition readily.

If this card comes up to indicate an alteration in a person's behavior, it will generally indicate a man moving into and feeling somewhat troubled by a new romantic relationship. The Knight is the card that comes up to indicate a man happily falling in love.

Look for surrounding cards to clarify whether any misgivings are justified—for instance, the Moon or the 7 of Cups would be warnings of danger; also look at whether cards like the 7 of Swords or the 7 of Disks come up—these may indicate inner personal worries that will only cause problems if allowed to.

Bottom Line Interpretations (Tarantino): Listen to your passions and then let those feelings guide you. Even though your emotions run deep, you don't always choose to express them. Such powerful feelings, when tempered by self-discipline, are great assets for achieving your goals. Wanting, wishing, and desiring are necessary ingredients in any creative activity. Negative: calm down and think before acting. Surface appearances are unreliable and should not be trusted. Your communication with others may be experienced as too intense since you rarely share your feelings or assert yourself. Consider whether your expectations are realistic.

Advice: Central task is becoming aware of and learning to master dealing with emotional needs. To do so, wishes and desires must be perceived and recognized as they are the fundamental driving forces in our lives.

PRINCESS OF CUPS

TAROTNYMS

Pure of heart/innocence/guileless versus faint of heart/fragile/unaware of own power

Uninhibited/fearless diving in versus dependent

Evocative/sensitive/appealing versus impulsive/secretive/unreal

ELEMENTAL SNAPSHOT

THE DAUGHTER OF THE FLOOD
(EMOTIONAL INNONCENCE)

MAIN SUMMARY MEANING:

The earthy part of water. Grace, sweetness, gentleness, helpmeet, kindness and tenderness, living in a world of dreamer/romance/rapture. Fragile in dealing with harsher realities of life. Dependent on others but also helpful.

SYMBOLISM:

- Element = Water;
- Rosy mantle is a symbol of a gentle, loving nature;
- Jewels on her gown indicate love, kindness, and generosity;
- Earthy part of water means that she crystalizes her intuition, imagination, and feelings in a material way through acts of love, generosity, and kindness;
- We see her dancing on the water, bringing her dreams into manifestation, uninhibited in expressing her emotions;

- The seashell represents imagination, intuition, dreams and feelings;
- The swan, rising above her head, shows the freedom she feels to love and express herself;
- The turtle emerging from the shell represent her commitment and reliability in a relationship;
- The dolphin is a symbol of well-being for the pure of heart;
- With her outstretched arm she welcomes;
- The white lotus in her hand represents purity of intention, love without condition;
- The color blue symbolizes loving wisdom; pink, innocence and beauty; green, creativity.

DIVINATION:

The person is ready to love. Sometimes this card comes up to indicate forthcoming pregnancy. The card also appears to indicate a woman falling in love. She is at peace with her emotional nature, often highly creative and artistic. She has a certain fragility, particularly when coming into contact with the harsher realities of everyday life, and will not always cope well with conflict. In her world, tranquility and harmony are highly valued.

Bottom Line Interpretations (Tarantino): To achieve your goals, you must be willing to remain in the background. If its appreciation you seek, you are likely to be disappointed. The situation at hand will demand considerable self-sacrifice and hard work. Learn how to support others without diminishing yourself. Negative: at this point in your life, you want full recognition you deserve. However, you're apprehensive about taking a chance on standing up and asking for what you need and claiming credit for your accomplishment. Until now, you've been willing to do more for others than for yourself. You'll find success if you be yourself without any pretense.

Advice: Listen carefully to the voice of your own intuition, and to follow through on any ideas which arise from it.

 SWORDS:

The element of the air, standing for the intellectual, mental condition, the logical and scientific (world of Yetzirah):

- Most subject to disturbance;
- We are repeatedly challenged to prove that what has been achieved on this level is real;
- Can also indicate/show what energies we are using (usually unconsciously) to shape our lives.

The element of Air is the pure mind, the thought and the intellect, synthesis and analysis, the proceeding of the amorphous spirit of Fire and the unconscious emotion of Water into definitions and concepts. Air is both structure and conscious realization, both formation and abstraction.

Air is best described with Descartes, "Cogito ergo sum" — I think, therefore I am, and in a further step, "Dubito, ergo cogito, ergo sum" — I doubt, therefore I think, therefore I am. Air does not exist beyond its own thinking, the very processes of its ever busy mind ARE its existence. If the thinking ever stops Air ceases to exist. At the same time, Air is movement, free flow, and unrestricted freedom. Just try and stop your mind from thinking, realizing, formulating, reacting - you'll find it will never work.

So Air is no artificial instrument - it is rather a basic principle of all existence. As long as there is life there is thought, without thought, the being would not even be aware of its own existence. Both the Spirit of Fire and the Emotion of Water need the thought to emulate the mere instinct to a conscious realization.

Air in its substance is all around us, it manifests in the breath that is the ultimate precondition for life, it is the carrier for all sound, and it is the wind culminating from the heating of the poles and the rotation of the earth. Air can be a gentle breeze and a ferocious, destructive storm.

The Greeks connected Air even with the Aether, as 'aer' meaning the lower atmosphere and 'aether' the distant upper atmosphere above the clouds.

Some people wondered why from all elements Air was connected with the Sword. A sword is a weapon - and a sophisticated weapon as that. For a long time, producing good swords was an art, much effort was put in the forging of the blade which had to be perfect in material and balance. And all that work went into the construction of a thing used for killing.

Killing in general is not specific to Air–when in a fit of rage someone grabs a club and strikes it is more a matter of Fire. Yet, the art of killing, the mindset behind a war, the planning of a battle –all this requires a mind making up the reasoning for this.

ACE OF SWORDS

TAROTNYMS

Creative energy/transformation/goal-directed/start of something new versus thought without clear plan or practical application

Intellectual clarity/seeing things clearly/cutting through confusion or misdirection/decisive versus belligerence/blunt/cruel

Taking time to think carefully/be balanced versus unfair/unbalanced/swayed by irrelevances or self interest

ELEMENTAL SNAPSHOT

THE ROOT OF CONSCIOUSNESS (PURE THOUGHT)

MAIN SUMMARY MEANING:

The root of the powers of the Air. Power for good and evil. Conquest, force, activity, strength, just punishment.

SYMBOLISM:

- The obvious symbol of Air is wind, which blows wherever it blows. It's all embracing, all wandering, all penetrating, and all consuming;

- The card represents the sword of Magus (card 1), crowned with 22 rays of light, signifying Kether (the highest realm on the Tree of Life). Inscribed on the sword is the Greek word, "Thelema, or "Will." It is a symbol of creative energy brought about by intellectual clarity. The sword thrusts forward, through patterns of thought seeking truth, light displacing the dark clouds of mind. The grip is a coiled snake, symbol of transformation, along with two crescent shaped moons, showing that unconscious energies are become accessible to consciousness.

DIVINATION:

The ability to see things from a clear perspective, cut away the rubbish and confusion, and see what is important and worth fighting for. We can also identify the red herrings that keep us from seeing clearly.

We become more able to make good decisions. Energies are fully available for use. We have success over difficulties, the start of something new.

Bottom Line Interpretations (Tarantino): You are in a good position to cut through the uncertainty that has surrounded you/your situation. As confusion clears, your mind will be focused and it will be easier to cultivate new ideas. You have a clear shot at success if you are willing to orchestrate your thoughts, attitudes, and believes into a single-minded focus on your goals. Negative: Your thinking is unclear at the moment. Wait until the dust settles before proceeding. Take care not to be distracted or pressured by other people. Proceed only when you are clear about what you want and how to go about creating it. Precision, organization, and attention to detail are required.

Advice: Step back, and think rationally. Cut away rubbish and clutter, give into the force you are feeling to get started and move forward. Follow three steps: (1) write down your goal; (2) be clear about the desired outcome; and (3) strive to think in an innovative, creative, and independent manner.

Every now and again, the Ace of Swords will come up as the Sword of Justice. When you find yourself in this situation, be very careful about the judgments you make. To be just requires that you are totally balanced. This is the only way that you are able to make choices based on the actual issues at hand, without being swayed or influenced by irrelevancies.

TWO OF SWORDS: PEACE

TAROTNYMS

Calm/peace/tranquility versus a storm approaching/peace but not victory/tension remains

Reconciliation/resolution/using thought to resolve a hopeless situation versus adopting simplified (binary thinking)/giving in to move forward/intolerable compromise

Settlement of conflict/reaching a middle point between extremes versus détente/lack of growth/needing to take the high ground

ELEMENTAL SNAPSHOT

THE SPIRIT OF BALANCE (CONCEPTUAL RECONCILATION)

MAIN SUMMARY MEANING:

Contradictory characteristics in the same nature. Sacrifice and trouble giving birth to strength. Quarrel made up and peace restored, although tension remains. Pleasure after pain.

SYMBOLISM:

- Zodiac = Libra (sign of Balance); Planet = Moon (inner, imagination, unconscious, reflective, illusive, emotion);

- Two swords are united by a blue rose (representing, since pierced, that which is not attainable) with five petals, emanating white rays symbolizing energy beyond the disruption of the intellect. Their geometric pattern represents equilibrium, like a propeller they show freshness and movement. The praying figures on the handles pray for peace;

- The two small swords, one with the moon representing emotions; the other the sign of Libra, representing balance. In all, the picture symbolizes having made a decision and temporarily found some piece of mind. The four pinwheels signify that the mind gives form and structure to all four aspects of life (mental, physical, spiritual, emotional). Yellow symbolizes intellectual development, green the energy of reorganization.

DIVINATION:

The card often comes up to indicate that a conflict has been resolved or a breach healed, so there will have been trouble earlier on. Friendships are rebuilt, old wounds are healed. However in this context it is very important to look carefully at the cards which follow it, for there is often a feeling that a relationship will never be quite the same again as it was before the conflict or quarrel. It marks the period of tranquility and calmness that can arise when we have finally made difficult decisions, and acted upon them. Often it will come up to show that, now we have got to grips with our confusion, we can rest and recover.

The two small swords, one with the moon representing emotions; the other the sign of Libra, representing balance.

Bottom Line Interpretations (Tarantino): You can no longer avoid making a decision. Neither can you leave the responsibility to someone else. Take your time and listen to your rational mind as well as your intuition. Once made, don't second guess yourself. The pressure will lift and you'll feel a renewed sense of purpose. Negative: It's hard not to second guess yourself, especially when everyone around you has a different opinion about what to do. Focus on what's best and most comfortable for you. Give some thought to the possibility that you don't need to reach a decision at this exact moment.

Advice: If there are any issues about which you feel emotionally sore and unhappy, make a deliberate and conscious effort to get to the high ground, above the situation.

The card will also come up to show that we have let go of old fears or anxieties that were holding us back. It's a still card indicating a time to rest and recuperate.

THREE OF SWORDS: SORROW

TAROTNYMS

Clarity is disrupted versus think clearly before acting/don't sweat the small stuff/things seem larger than they are (worse/more catastrophic) at the time/don't catastrophize/all storms pass/mastery of care and worry/development of shrewd insight

Loss or separation/dispute or deceit by a third party versus facing problems head on/avoiding cynicism/moving beyond disappointment

A decision or choice must be made but clarity is obstructed by doubt/fear/worry or one feels unable/uncertain how to tackle versus being unable prolongs the worry and uncertainty/the situation would resolve if a decision were made/address problems directly

ELEMENTAL SNAPSHOT

THE SPIRIT OF DEJECTION
(CONSCIOUS DISAPPOINTMENT)

MAIN SUMMARY MEANING:

Sorrow, melancholy, unhappiness, tears, disruption, discord, delay, sorry, losses, absence, endings/disputes or separation, deceit (involving a third party).

SYMBOLISM:

- Zodiac = Libra (sign of balance); Planet = Saturn (slow, heavy, obstinate);
- The great sword of the magician, points up, meeting (cutting) at the junction of two swords, indicating that the sword of clarity (will) is being obstructed by the two smaller swords which are bent (out of harmony). Together, the swords destroy the golden rose—symbolizing completeness or harmony. Injured, it drops its pedals symbolizing tears from the heart of humankind. The background shows a storm, symbolizing clouds of doubt, fear, and worry. The crescent moons and solar disks tell us to allow sorrow to surface so that we can begin to process it. The snake represents the need to shed the old (release the sorrow), and move back into balance.

DIVINATION:

The 3 of Swords will almost always indicate loss or separation. It represents the pattern of action following the pattern of thought from the previous card—the 2 of Swords (indicating peace through compromise and struggle). In order to determine how serious this is liable to be, you need to consider the cards surrounding this one. And often during times like this, there are choices and decisions to be made, which you feel too uncertain to tackle. Yet the fact that you are unable to make your decisions perhaps prolongs a difficult or unsatisfactory situation, adding to your anxiety and worry.

May indicate a tension filled relationship with a third party, attempting to destroy the relationship.

Bottom Line Interpretations (Tarantino): This is a time of new beginnings, a time to confront your grief (loss, sorrow), and move on. Stop waiting for the worst, doubting yourself, and rehashing the past. It is essential to adopt a beginners mind, unburdened by past success or failure. Negative: the chaos of late is beginning to settle down. Your experiences have given you the knowledge necessary to make wiser choices going forward. There is no need to relive painful memories. Work at creating a new history. From this point on life will get easier.

Advice: The lesson to be learned here is the mastery of care and worry. A brooding, distrustful outlook must be recognized clearly as negative energy separating us from our origins.

Do not avoid the problems in the relationship that is currently tension filled as it will only lead to sorrow and worry. Address secrets, explore unhappy feelings, wonder if there are issues that we are feeling unable to deal with, which are causing us pain or confusion. However, it's important not to expect ourselves to deal with conflicts or problems until we feel stronger.

FOUR OF SWORDS: TRUCE

TAROTNYMS

Stability returns versus problems postponed/temporary respite or truce

Peace achieved/possibility of peace via strength or sacrifice versus no real resolution/constant vigilance

Time to think, generate new awareness/ideas/"bury the hatchet" versus putting problems on hold/enjoying the respite/acting "as if" the problems are "out there"

ELEMENTAL SNAPSHOT

THE SPIRIT OF CONTEMPLATION
(CONSCIOUS BALANCE/STALEMATE)

MAIN SUMMARY MEANING:

Worries have been conquered, clarity regained, albeit temporary respite or truce.

SYMBOLISM:

- Zodiac = Libra (sign of balance); Planet = Jupiter (sign of luck and expansion);
- The four swords (representing an impasse) are at the corner of St. Andrew's cross (symbol of suffering and martyrdom), their points sheathed in a rose (symbol of harmony) of 49 pedals, representing the establishment of dogma and convention in matters of intellect;
- The light blue color represents the temporary calmness. The yellow lines indicate that nothing has really changed. Green behind each sword represents the creativity of that chosen direction.

DIVINATION:

A temporary respite, often after we have passed through trying times. This is a quiet period, which should be used to recover, regroup and stabilize. It's important though, that we always bear in mind the fact that this is only a moment in time. Soon we shall be required to pick up the tools of life and continue on our journey. The apparent stability of the four meeting swords means that we will suffer until we look inward for the solution.

Whatever situation that, before, seemed hopeless contains the elements for a fortunate, prosperous solution.

Bottom Line Interpretations (Tarantino): Stop trying to push a square peg in a round hole. It is in your best interest to negotiate a compromise. Flexibility and cooperation will establish a productive flow in communication. Now is the time to withdraw and regroup. In the meantime, engage in activities that have nothing to do with the current situation/struggle. Negative: in an effort to keep the peace, you've been making too many concessions, compromising what you believe in. Think about why you might be too afraid to speak your mind and stand up for yourself. If you don't sell yourself short you'll get what you want.

Advice: Truce does not mean peace. Consider whether surface calm masks suppressed feelings and impulses. This is a respite—a down time in which we can catch our breath, ease our tension and relax for a brief time. But once that has been done, we need to recognize that there is still more to be done—the battle isn't over yet. So when acting under the influence of this card, bear in mind that first you must take it easy, but then you must begin to plan your next step. If we fail to do that then, when the effect of the truce passes, we shall be left high and dry, with no route planned for our future. And in that case the turmoil which preceded this card may well manifest again. May need to "bury the hatchet" with someone.

FIVE OF SWORDS: DEFEAT

TAROTNYM

Making room for objectivity/clarity (blue border) versus being overcome with fear and negativity/destructive thinking

Need for renewal, awareness, energy versus rumination/brooding/return of old wounds/cowardice

Acceptance of one's own limits/failures versus defeat/denial

Failure always precedes growth/standing tall in the face of attacks versus defeat as a result of exaggerated avoidance of conflicts

ELEMENTAL SNAPSHOT

THE SPIRIT OF HUMILATION (CONSCIOUS SETBACK)

MAIN SUMMARY MEANING:

Defeat, loss, malice, spite, weakness, slander, failure, anxiety, poverty, dishonor, trouble, grief, ties, gossip, interference, cowardice.

SYMBOLISM:

- Zodiac = Aquarius (sign of freedom through discipline); Planet = Venus (sign of love and beauty);
- The hilts of the swords form an inverted pentagram (symbol of humans), similar in shape to Atu 12, "Hanged Man" (see also Atu 13, "Death," and 16, "The Tower"), indicating life turned upside down;

- The blades are broken and crooked typifying intellect enfeebled by sentiment. Blood symbolizing old wounds, bleeding anew. Each sword represents a different aspect of the situation. The fish represents the past; the sleeping snake, a lack of renewal; the downward crown, lost awareness; the ram's horn, the lack of new impulses; the seashell, the need for protection. The rose (harmony) is gone, leaving only the pedals;
- The blue border symbolizes objectivity and clarity. The yellow and green colors suggest that with time and objectivity, healing will come. The challenge is to make room for this despite overwhelming feelings of fear.

DIVINATION:

Fear of defeat dominates the moment, maybe connected with relationships, more generally of something that is of great importance to the person. May experience a lack of control.

Bottom Line Interpretations (Tarantino): Time to examine your core beliefs about success and failure. Don't let doubt rule your mental world. Set goals that are realistic. Stop thinking of yourself as a victim. Your desire to succeed must override your expectation or history of failure. Negative: you may not have control over specific events/circumstances, but you to have power over your thoughts. Don't let pride stand in your way of trying again. Use the opposition you experience to strengthen your determination.

Advice: You might get news that you don't want, or have one of your hopes dented a bit. If that is the case, don't turn that disappointment into fear. Spend some time with your feelings. You are entitled to feel let down when something that matters to you goes awry. Do something gentle to remind yourself of the things which are right in your life, and then dust off your disappointment, and decide which course of action will serve you best in order to try to follow through on what you need.

Very often, when we get knocked back, we compound it by beating ourselves up. In no time at all, the original disappointment has been overwhelmed by a bunch of other negative thoughts and attitudes that hurt and damage us. By the time we've finished we are desperately distressed, have harmed our self-esteem, and feel completely incapable of contributing anything useful or worthwhile.

Evaluate whether the failure is one of your own making, a part of the journey toward a better, more meaningful life. Examining one's failures as sources of knowledge is the first step toward recovery. At the same time, if due to a relationship, the heartless, hate, embittered, and lust for power of those involved will require that one martial all subliminal, aggressive energy and allow it to erupt all at once.

SIX OF SWORDS: SCIENCE

TAROTNYMS

Balance and integration, feeling of wholeness/understanding versus stuck in outdated models and ways of thinking

Clarity or the ability to analyze with clarity/sharp focus versus longing for liberation through knowledge

A new, encompassing vision/coming together/synthesis versus setting off for/or need to set off for new shores/drive for freedome

Approaching problems with rationality and objectivity versus emotions/prejudices/mistrust

ELEMENTAL SNAPSHOT

THE SPIRIT OF KNOWLEDGE
(CONSCIOUS INTEGRATION)

MAIN SUMMARY MEANING:

Science. A perfect balance of mental and moral faculties, hard won and impossible to hold. Search for truth. Drive for freedom, long for liberation through knowledge.

SYMBOLISM:

- Zodiac = Aquarius (sign of freedom through discipline); planet = Mercury (will and swiftness);

- The hilts of the swords form a hexagon, their points touch the outer pedals of a red rose (heart) in the middle of a Golden Cross of six squares (harmony). All pointing in one direction, the six swords symbolize the power of mind focused in one direction. Both the rose and the cross symbolize the secret of scientific truth which repeatedly forces us to break away from outdated models and ways of thinking. The lines in the background show that there is abundant activity. The circle inside the square is a symbol of wholeness and stability. Since they are drawn lightly, they highlight the transient nature of intellectual structures.

DIVINATION:

The ability to analyze brings clarity about the future. The most varied ideas and visions meet at one central point. A new and encompassing vision brings the rose of realization to bloom.

We perceive ourselves as the messenger of the spirit of our times, courier of a new age, and bearer of a higher order, sense the urge to let others take part in this knowledge.

Ability to mediate and communicate in a way that reduces conflicts through synthesis.

Optimal balance between emotional needs and concepts of mind. Good time to build and expand a harmonious relationship.

Bottom Line Interpretations (Tarantino): Balance and integration have been achieved. From here, you can open your mind to new possibilities. Be inquisitive and ask as many questions as you can. Include honest reflections about your mistakes so they reveal what to avoid. Negative: when you become emotionally involved, you risk losing the objectivity needed for clear thinking. You are only seeing and hearing what you want, thereby eliminating the chance for creative solutions. Listen to yourself and others. Check in regularly to ensure you really understand what is happening.

Advice: Analyze old ways of thinking, embrace new. We shall see things clearly, get issues into sharp focus and perhaps establish new perspectives. We must strive to climb for the higher ground, so as to get an overview on life which allows us to see its overall pattern. Problems must be approached rationally, and objectively. Emotional swings will be better curbed than indulged. Thus we shall find new and different solutions to difficulties. Communicate to others the changes that are needed.

SEVEN OF SWORDS: FUTILITY

TAROTNYMS

Recognition that ideas/goals/needs are not likely to succeed versus giving up/giving in/or getting off the path

Shrewd, sly, cleaver, crafty, diplomatic versus deceitful, intrigues, insincerity, dubious methods

Attempting to solve problems/make progress with careful thought versus sense of pointless/senselessness

ELEMENTAL SNAPSHOT

THE SPIRIT OF FLUCTUATION (CONSCIOUS OPPOSITION)

MAIN SUMMARY MEANING:

Futility, vacillation, wish to compromise, vain striving against opposition to powerful. Partial success. Fascination with display. Tendency to prefer the simple but deceptive answers to the truth.

SYMBOLISM:

- Zodiac = Aquarius (sign of freedom through discipline); Planet = Moon (inner, imagination, unconscious, reflective, illusive, emotion);

- Here the sword of clarity (with Sun on the hilt) is attacked by smaller swords each with a planetary symbol on its hilt: sun and moon have changed places, gloomy subconscious expectations muddy awareness; Neptune, everything is clouded by a film; Venus, it's too good to be true; Mars, I don't have the energy; Jupiter, there's too much good at once; Mercury, I can't convey it properly; Saturn, it's too much trouble;

- The large blade symbolizes the intellectual sharpness of separating and ordering, making a single course of action possible. The smaller swords are the unconscious shadows of this power (trickery, intrigues, shrewdness, untruthfulness, life's lies, and betrayal);
- The background color and shapes represent the fragility of the intellect.

DIVINIZATION:

There is a contest between the one strong and the merely feeble. We refuse to believe certain perceptions and shrink away from conflicts, in such situations perhaps choosing to trick others to get the best of them, but only hurting ourselves.

Bottom Line Interpretations (Tarantino): So much is happening, you are feeling overwhelmed. In truth, it's neither hopeless nor out of control. You are progressing according to plan. Create short term goals. Focus on what needs to be done today. Negative: Life is currently full of tests and challenges. It's time to experiment with different beliefs and ideas to determine which work best for you. Strive for competency rather than perfection. Procrastination is nothing more than self-doubt canceling out your natural drive. Choose not to listen. In the long run, you will develop healthy self-reliance.

Advice: Don't take the destructive thoughts seriously. We are often ready to make unsuitable compromises in order to try to ease the pressure we experience. We can be more easily impressed by other people's opinions, seeking to please them, often at our own expense. We vacillate, unable to stick to any decision we make. And all of this does nothing much more than increase our problems. Neither of these options is viable, if we are to live a happy love-filled life. We need to be prepared to commit ourselves to a course of action and then follow through. Even if it transpires that the choice we make could have been better, any choice is better than no choice at all, when the alternative is total inertia.

EIGHT OF SWORDS: INTERFERENCE

TAROTNYMS

Perception and will are blocked temporarily versus lack of persistence/giving up/losing sight of the goal

Caught up in minutiae/losing sight of the bigger picture/long term goal/objective versus having a variety of interests/seeing the forest and the trees

Easily distracted from the plan versus staying focused

Subject to criticism and opposition from others/meddling from usually supportive people/wrench thrown into the works versus sticking to the plan as it is good

ELEMENTAL SNAPSHOT

THE SPIRIT OF RESTLESSNESS (CONSCIOUS DISTRACTION)

MAIN SUMMARY MEANING:

Interferences, fragmentation, lack of persistence in intellectual matters. Delays are temporary rather than permanent.

SYMBOLISM:

- Zodiac = Gemini (sign of duality); Planet = Jupiter (sign of luck and expansion);

- Two strong central swords (will and perception) are crossed by six scimitars (roadblocks), three going each way, indicating that the straightness of the two swords is disturbed by the crosswise ones, symbolic of restlessness and confusion of thought (Gemini) that distracts people from the higher objectives (Jupiter). The wings in the background illustrate frustration.

DIVINATION:

You find yourself between two alternatives of apparently equal merit. Doubts and fears interfere with inner clarity. It is easy to give up, fail to endure.

At best, the 8 of Swords will indicate a period where nothing goes quite the way you want it to. At worst it will indicate an obstructive and difficult period where serious damage can be done to our material environment, our emotional balance and our overall sense of well-being.

Bottom Line Interpretations (Tarantino): You need to confront your doubts and deal with the mental confusion obscuring your path. The confusion originates in your mental attitude and believes. Negative: you are being held prisoner by your own thoughts and limiting beliefs. Admit the need to change, take responsibility for the changes you need to make, monitor and counter any self-defeating thoughts, and keep your thoughts on your goals.

Advice: First to try to isolate the source of the problem—inner or outer. Keep your eyes open for anyone else who may be deliberately stepping in your path. Often when somebody interferes, merely recognizing what they are doing robs their actions of any power over us.

NINE OF SWORDS: CRUELTY

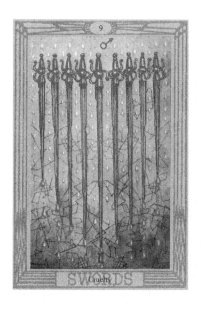

TAROTNYMS

People/circumstances torment us versus taking active steps to separate ourselves from them/standing up to them

Undoing something or making amends through atonement, martyrdom, devotion versus acceptance of martyrdom

Fear, guilt feelings, cruelty directed inward versus self-acceptance and understanding

Lack of reason/intellect replacing heartless (cruel) passion/fanaticism versus justice and mercy

ELEMENTAL SNAPSHOT

THE SPIRIT OF THE INQUISITION (THOUGHTLESS BRUTALITY)

MAIN SUMMARY MESSAGE:

Cruelty, intellect replaced with heartless passion, although still intellectual in form, the temper is of an inquisitor.

SYMBOLISM:

- Zodiac = Gemini (sign of duality); Planet = Mars (sign of aggression and power);
- Nine swords of different lengths point downward, rusted and chipped, poison blood dropping from their jagged points. The background is

studded with tears and crystal forms, the color heavy, dull, and lifeless. Clarity has disintegrated. Reason has been abandoned.

DIVINATION:

Generally means cruelty directed at yourself. Often, this card will be a comment on your own treatment of yourself—if you denigrate yourself and beat yourself up, you are facing the worst enemy of your life. Others' harshness likely continues. The card can come up to indicate some other person's cruelty toward you—in which case look for 'people' cards to give you a clue as to the instigator.

Bottom Line Interpretations (Tarantino): You have been caught in a cycle of hopelessness and despair. Connecting your self-worth to your present feelings is making matters worse. You need to work at regaining your sense of reason and objectivity. Your current circumstances and state of mind are not related to nor reflect on your fundamental character. Negative: success in this world is basically a matter of getting up more times than you fall down. Stop seeing yourself as a victim. Take full responsibility for altering the course of your circumstances.

Advice: Passive resistance, resignation, acceptance of martyrdom.

TEN OF SWORDS: RUIN

TAROTNYMS

Current views lead to ruin versus possibility of something new if one can be freed of old ways of thinking

Disenchantment versus nothing left to lose so might as well risk a new beginning

All intellectual development must push beyond/leave what came before in order build new understanding versus giving up /resignation

Ending of a relationship/way of thinking/path of development/possibly painfully or negative versus hanging on until it is too late

ELEMENTAL SNAPSHOT

THE SPIRIT OF NEGATION/WILL TO LIVE (CONSCIOUS CHANGE)

MAIN SUMMARY MEANING:

Ruin, faulty reasoning, death, failure, disruption, clever, eloquent, but impertinent person. Completion, end of a cycle. Spiritually, may herald the end of delusion.

SYMBOLISM:

- Zodiac = Gemini (sign of duality); Planet = Sun;
- The ten swords are arranged in the tree of life, but the points one to five, and seven to nine, shatter the central sword which represent Sun, the Heart.

The background is aflame with explosive destruction. The card shows reason run mad and a riot of soulless mechanism. The sun's energy is being directed into negative aspects of the intellect/mind;

- The number 10 always represents the culmination of energy. Like Death (XIII), and the Tower (XVI), it indicates a conclusion, ending, either by letting go, or like Aeon (XX), a new beginning or renewal.

DIVINATION:

The card shows the destructive power of constant negative thinking. Negativity disrupts and destroys the soul's natural striving toward harmony and balance. Possible difficulties in external conditions, including finances.

Bottom Line Interpretations (Tarantino): Your thoughts are getting the best of you. Your uneasiness not only affects your judgment but if ignored may make you physically ill. Monitor your thoughts and emotions carefully. Avoid projecting problems. Negative: the vague fear that has haunted you is dissipating. Conflicts also appear to be coming to an end. Soon you'll be able to relax and appreciate the changes that are occurring.

Advice: If we have believed in our worthiness to achieve and attain; if we have struggled to reach the highest limits of our own current spiritual potential; if we have lived in an ethical and fair manner, we will inevitably have attracted joy, happiness and success into our lives. If, on the other hand, we have fallen short of our best; believed in our weakness and therefore empowered that belief; if we have given in to negative and harmful thoughts, we will inevitably attract to us sadness, distrust and a reason to fear.

It is essential to somehow break out of the downward spiral. Positive thinking is a habit. So is negative thinking. And, as with all habits, it can be very challenging to change the pattern. Constant vigilance is required. We need to monitor our thoughts and feelings VERY carefully. And as soon as we discover that we are starting to think dark thoughts we need to pounce, snatching that thought up and determining where it has come from.

This applies as much to our deepest inner responses as it does to our responses to external stimuli. Life is always throwing the curve ball at you, just to see if you can catch it. And harmonizing yourself with the rhythm of life is—besides being the greatest reward of all—a very big challenge.

KNIGHT OF SWORDS

TAROTNYMS

Able to discern matters and change them/quick thinking/presence of mind versus bitter and cynical criticism

Intellectually astute versus emotionally unaware (cold)/disconnected or appearing cunning and phony (salesman/entrepreneur)/sophistry versus sincerity

Super rational (philosopher/mathematician)/charming/word smith/reliance on intellectual concepts versus mind games/can twist words/silver tongued (diplomat/lawyer)

Comfortable in contradictions as the world is mostly intellectual concepts versus fickle/difficult to pin down/game player

ELEMENTAL SNAPSHOT

THE FATHER OF PERCEPTION (CONSCIOUS DYNAMISM)

MAIN SUMMARY MEANING:

The fiery part of air. The will and intent of the mind. Active man, astute, intelligent, skillful and clever. Able to analyze and discern things as they are and change them. Fierce and courageous, but possibly emotionally unreflective. Can have difficulty with highly emotional people.

SYMBOLISM:

- Element = Air;
- Zodiac = Gemini;
- The Knight is on a golden horse, in gold-green armor, riding at full gallop, symbolizing passionate, creative, and unbridled, goal-oriented, mental activity, and strong mental concentration;
- The four transparent wings indicate that the Knight can move in any direction: mental, physical, spiritual, emotional;
- The six pointed star at the center of the wings stands for clarity;
- The three swallows alongside are symbols of body, intellect, and spirit;
- Yet, both he and the birds are above the water (emotion), indicating perhaps being above or disconnected from emotion, in the heights of thought;
- Two swords indicate yang (male, long, logic) and yin (female, short, receptivity) energy;
- The four propellers on his helmet signify his capacity to look at matters from all angles and change his mind easily if new data calls for a different conclusion;
- The speed of the blue clouds symbolizes how quickly mind (air) moves and changes.

DIVINATION:

Thoughts and ideas come at lightning speed. Imaginative and flexible thinking is used to achieve goals.

You'll finding yourself thinking quickly and clearly, finding unexpected solutions to apparently intractable problems. Matters which had, until now, refused to yield solutions, will suddenly start willingly spitting them out, so you can clear several obstacles from your path.

In relationships, excitement may be more prominent or interesting than emotional depth, devotion, and emotional merging. Fear of losing one's self may be driving the situation.

Bottom Line Interpretations (Tarantino): Think before you speak to avoid unintentionally offending or intimidating people. Because you analyze information quickly, you must make an effort to be patient with others who think more slowly. Spend some time gathering new information. If you suspend judgment until you've gathered enough data and looked at all the facts, you'll know exactly what to do when the time comes to proceed. Negative: you risk "chasing your tail" until you know for sure what you want. When you are uncertain, it's easy to strike out at someone who is trying to help you. If you are willing to use the information others give you, your indecision will end and progress will be made.

Advice: Pick out the things which have been giving you headaches in the last little while. Spend a little time (not too much) considering the apparent obstacles and difficulties of the problem. Then forget it! At some point during the day, a solution should quite simply pop into your head. Also keep a close watch on your dreams overnight—these may contain the answers you seek.

QUEEN OF SWORDS

TAROTNYMS

Graceful/perceptive/attractive versus superficial and phony

Abundance of ideas/quick and razor sharp perception/able to get to the heart of the matter versus calculating and cool

Brings the power of mind, reason, intellect, rationality to the emotional realm/unhampered by emotion/independent versus distant/castrating

Willingness to learn/conduct ourselves frankly and with open eyes and gracefulness versus dominating, cruel/needing to prove a point

ELEMENTAL SNAPSHOT

MOTHER OF LIGHT AND EMOTIONAL WISDOM (CONSCIOUSLY PERCEPTIVE)

MAIN SUMMARY MEANING:

The watery part of air. A graceful, perceptive woman, proud and dignified, a keen observer, and subtle interpreter with childlike curiosity. Confident and gracious, can be superficially attractive which makes her dangerous as she can cut right to the heart of the matter.

SYMBOLISM:

- Zodiac = Libra;
- Element = Air;
- The sword of clarity cuts through the masks one wears, leaving one open and receptive;
- The Queen possesses highly honed intuition. She is acutely analytical, with a razor-sharp ability to get to the heart of a situation, seeing exactly what is, rather than what others would wish her to see. Her naked chest indicates her openness and compassion;
- The sword and large, bearded male head symbolizes both liberation and independence from old ideas and traditions. She is able to separate intellect from reactivity;
- The crystals behind her head symbolize the flowing of ideas into form as well as the ability to see clearly and rationally;
- The helmet has the head of a child, indicating renewal and creativity as well as curiosity and innocence in the search for truth;
- Being enthroned on a cloud means she is able to sit back and be a detached observer;
- The blue sky symbolizes tranquility.

DIVINATION:

Penetrating insight will often reveal aspects of themselves to others that they had previously been unable to grasp—thus she is a capable therapist, teacher or leader.

The woman represented by this card will be experienced in the flow of life, understanding a great deal about both the great triumphs, and the deepest failings of life. Her clarity and measured expression will be of great value at times of confusion and sadness. The more negative aspects of the Queen—coldness, judgmental, criticism. At these times there is a certain sourness about her, with cynicism and sharpness making themselves felt.

Bottom Line Interpretations (Tarantino): Put your feelings aside for the time being and think with your head. Examine any ties with the past that may negatively influence your judgment and present circumstances. Look behind the façade and "cut to the chase." Negative: the time has come to set aside past anger and resentment. Approach the present with kindness and consideration. A little compassion and understanding will help you realize your dreams.

Advice: We need to practice our own powers of perception. Rather than dealing with the psychic quality which is rightly the realm of the Queen of Cups, we must now turn our attention to the everyday world. Try to remind yourself to study the interactions you have with others. Don't just deal with the face value. Struggle to seek behind that mask for the whole being beyond.

PRINCE OF SWORDS

TAROTNYMS

New ideas/thoughts/brainstorming/plans/overcoming obstacles versus flighty/distracted/erratic/hasty/impractical

Spontaneous/enthusiastic versus unpredictable/eternal adolescence/immature

Charismatic/dramatic/inspirational versus smart aleck, know-it-all/always building castles in the air/hot air

ELEMENTAL SNAPSHOT

THE SON OF PERCEPTION
(CONSCIOUSLY EXCITEABLE)

MAIN SUMMARY MEANING:

The airy part of air. Leaping in the air. A young, intellectual man, full of ideas and designs, but unrelated to any practical effort. Able to argue any position, but not connected to any.

SYMBOLISM:

- Zodiac = Aquarius;
- Element = Air;
- Tight green armor symbolizing creativity in thinking and planning;
- Three figures (limiting forces) pull the wagon in diverse directions, making progress in any particular direction difficult.

- In the right hand a sword to create, in the left a sickle to immediately destroy whatever comes to mind;
- The reins loosely held in the hand symbolize freedom to think and create without effort, direction, or interference;
- The yellow spheres are a symbol for thought;
- The double diamond symbolizes perception becoming crystalized (think of the Fool [0]).

DIVINATION:

A highly intellectual and usually well-educated person, with a rapid fire mind and a great capacity for abstract thinking. He produces ideas with astonishing speed, but often moves on too quickly to follow through or elaborate on them. He can be challenging, entertaining, stimulating - and completely exhausting!

This card can indicate a phase of lightness where we are enthusiastic about new theoretical solutions. The "fresh wind" may be difficult to operationalize in reality.

The card represents a private person, who defends his inner space quite determinedly. This is someone who is hard to get to know—in fact, you'll probably not succeed entirely no matter how long you know him. He is a thinker, and chooses those he shares his thoughts with carefully. He's usually also very independent, and often appears unemotional and cold.

Bottom Line Interpretations (Tarantino): Determination to succeed. However, an abundance of ideas may block your path, making it difficult to choose and focus on one. Without a concrete agenda, boredom or chaos can enter the picture. Negative: beware of arrogance. Stop and think before jumping to conclusions. Broaden your perspective and deepen your understanding of the situation. Instead of confrontation,
try listening.

Advice: The speed with which new ideas occur, may lead to a lack of follow through. Take the time to carefully think and review each thought and idea.

PRINCESS OF SWORDS

TAROTNYMS

New ideas/clarity/insight replacing/disrupting/revolutionizing versus impulsivity/tempestuous/hasty/fragments

Breaking away/new ground versus adolescent rebellion

Telling things as they are without regard for the consequence/letting the chips fall where they may

Seeking to root out or coming into direct contact with injustice versus youthful idealism

ELEMENTAL SNAPSHOT

THE DAUGHTER OF REVOLUTION (CONSCIOUS IDEALISM)

MAIN SUMMARY MEANING:

The earthy (daughter) part of air (storm clouds). Logical, firm, aggressive, cunning, frivolous, rebellious, pious, manipulative. She is responsible for the materialization of an idea, practical. Great dexterity in the management of practice affairs, especially when they are of controversial nature. This card is another of those that has quite a bad reputation with some Tarot commentators—maybe because of her tendency to tell things as she sees them regardless of the consequences. Yet, unless she is badly dignified, the woman represented by this card will usually be honest, and frank.

SYMBOLISM:

- Element = Air;

- A young woman, stern and vengeful, with destructive logic, firm and aggressive, skilled in practical affairs. A keen observer, who brings clarity and insight to situations in which she is involved. She is a forceful and self-determining young woman who does not tolerate injustice, weakness and manipulation;

- She is probably not as secretive nor as hidden as some of the other Sword people—in fact, she tends to express her insight quite forcibly at times. She has the same qualities as a keen observer of life, and people, that we see in the other Sword Courts. She's also a skilled arbitrator, having extensive negotiating skills and a ruthless cutting edge;

- The sword pointed at the Earth means that she has the imposing responsibility of putting ideas into physical form. It's not an easy job—no matter what she does, she feels as if she always falls short of her original idea. She must cut through the clouds and keep trying;

- When intellectual ability meets earth, the altars of old ideas are destroyed, leaving room for eventual clarity;

- The dark clouds symbolize the struggle we must undertake if our ideas are ever to bear fruit;

- Helmet with medusa crest means that she can create fear in her enemies, turn them to stone with just a look.

DIVINATION:

Expect to come into contact with demanding or unfair situations. Use the clarity and insight offered by the card to cut away unnecessary rubbish, get behind the smoke-screens and see right to the heart of any situation that crosses your path.

Bottom Line Interpretations (Tarantino): It's time to stop talking about your ideas and act. Don't overanalyze. Trust your capacity to deal with problems in a direct, practical, and outspoken manner. There's bound to be a difference between your vision and the results. Be bold and fearless in your actions and daring in your quest to succeed. Negative: this is not a good time to be reticent. If you want to achieve your goals, you must take an active role. Don't let cynicism lead to inertia. You can't win if you don't try.

Advice: It is important to refuse to tolerate injustice or ill-treatment. That said, when you deal with situations such as this, be sure that your own responses and behavior are moral and above board, otherwise you'll find the Princess's sword turning on you.

It will be a day in which things are re-assessed, mulled over, straightened out. It may also be a day upon which unexpected and previously hidden things come to light. In this case, objectivity is the safest course of action, coupled with well-thought out action.

If you do not actually come into contact with a situation which demands you deal with it, be sure and spend a little time thinking about where you place importance on morality and good standards. Consider the things you see as 'right' and 'wrong, then check you're living up to those standards.

 DISKS:

The element of the earth, standing for the materials, the body, physical reality, the "down-to-earth-matters" (world of Assiah).

Dealings with the earth realm include health, nutrition, clothing, possessions, finances, poverty and wealth.

The Element of Earth is the essential matter, it is the most stable and fixed of the elements and has no mobility whatsoever. It is passive but solid, inflexible and concrete. It is ground and form and also the material body of living things.

The Earth is dry and cold, formative and determining. It is structuring and materializing. While Air and Fire ascend and Water descends, the Earth is fixed at the bottom; it is the secure, solid foundation of being, the ultimate physical body.

Earth is the element most depending on the other elements for Earth alone is dead and lifeless, rigid and cold, mere material without the trace of anything alive in it. It needs Water to be fertilized, Air to be animated, and Fire to be inspired. On the other hand, it is the most important base for all others to be grounded—therefore it is associated with Malkuth, called "the Kingdom" in the Tree of Life.

In the Kabbalah, Earth is associated with Nefesh—the "Animal Soul" and the world of Assiah which is the world of making, the world of action. It is the one world where all forms take place and are finally united, the spiritual principle of stable, inflexible synthesis, and the passive imposition of form.

At this point one should note that the Kabbalah actually does not equate the Earth with an element in the same vein as Fire, Water and Air. When we remember the nature of Malkuth it is not anything emanating from above but a fixed plane, the ultimate receiver where all emanations take their final form. It is root and origin because it is there where the physical, comprehensible existence actually begins to manifest.

As an example: figure you want to write something, an essay, a poem, a novel. Fire would represent your spirit to do so, Water would give depth and meaning to what you want to write, Air would provide the means to develop and structure your writing, put it into an eligible literary form. Earth would be the ink and the paper (or any other means required to transform your aspirations into actual, physical existence).

In Tarot, Earth is represented by the Disks, standing for all things material—which does not only mean "profane materials" but the actual body and form of our existence.

ACE OF DISKS

TAROTNYMS

Wealth and power versus questions about security, stability, endurance

Inner and outer brilliance/success/money versus dramatic change/new cycle

Potential/continuous development/progress in desired direction versus struggling with the values/meaning of our actions (inner versus outer development)

ELEMENTAL SNAPSHOT

THE POWER OF LIFE (EARTHLY POWER)

MAIN SUMMARY MEANING:

The roots of power of earth. Material gain, power, labor, wealth, contentment, materialism. Inner and outer richness, great success. Unification of body and soul, heaven and earth, sun and earth, wholeness.

SYMBOLISM:

- The symbols on this card are arranged in the shape of a cross representing the integration of the vertical and horizontal, inner and outer. Body and soul are united;
- Disks, according to Crowley, are whirling, like the planets in space;
- The number 6 refers to the sun. The 7-pointed star and two pentangles surround the symbol 1/666, representing the beast of the apocalypse, a

symbol for completion, the number 1, representing the Scarlet Woman in Atu XI, Lust). The words around the circle mean initiation or entrance;

- The angel wings symbolize continuous development, a readiness to live a life that is inwardly and outwardly rich.

DIVINATION:

Aces are always big influences, marking the beginning of something new and important. So if we see the card coming up to represent a sudden input of funds, expect this to cause major changes in the person's life.

A remarkably optimistic card, which usually heralds an exciting period of progress, whether spiritually or materially. We can expect expansion, new beginnings and often also, an input of funds. On the everyday level, the start of a new project, which is likely to be successful. So it will come up to show a new job, or a new business venture. Usually this will be the sort of project that seems to continuously keep on growing, with each level of attainment producing— almost of itself—the next step in the journey.

Sometimes the Ace will come up to indicate a sudden change of material fortune, or a windfall - though either of these would have to be quite substantial to invoke the Ace. There is a less obvious perspective on this card, too, which has to do with its inner truths. Disks are not only about money, physical life and materiality. They are also about the cycles of life, of the planet, and of ourselves.

Bottom Line Interpretations (Tarantino): Create a firm foundation before attempting to move ahead. The more grounded you are, the more able you'll be to bring your dreams to life. Negative: let go of your belief in scarcity. Start by making a list of everything in your life that you're grateful for. You must grow into the potential for abundance and prosperity.

Advice: Keep your eyes wide open for good opportunities to either start off new projects, or to engage more thoroughly with ongoing work.

TWO OF DISKS: CHANGE

TAROTNYMS

Change is constant/enriching/new goals or directions versus fear of loss/stagnation

Unity/connection/awareness of the alternation of opposites versus polarization/false distinctions

Awareness that all things have two sides/being aware of both sides/freeing one's self from one-sidedness

ELEMENTAL SNAPSHOT

THE CONTINUITY OF LIFE (EARTHLY CYCLES)

MAIN SUMMARY MEANING:

Change, harmony of change, alternation of gain and loss, weakness and strength, elation and melancholy. Varying occupation, wandering, visit to friends, pleasant change.

SYMBOLISM:

- Zodiac = Capricorn (sign of duty); Planet = Jupiter (luck/fortune);
- The snake is coiled into a figure 8, symbol of infinity indicating that change is constant and necessary. Lack of motion leads to decay. The crown is a symbol of wakefulness/awareness that change itself governs the earth, the status quo must be destroyed to make way for the new;
- The yin and yang symbols represent all life in harmonious motion, through the balance of opposites.

DIVINATION:

The card indicates the necessity of constant change in life if we are not to stagnate. It often marks a turning point—a new job, a shift of fortune, a move of home.

We do, though, often fear change in our lives. We will struggle against anything that appears to alter the pre-planned pattern we have applied to our future. But that's exactly what this card does—instigates change. Sometimes we think that the change is bad—and on the face of it, it may appear to be—yet whenever the 2 of Disks appears, it's warning us that change has become imperative. Something is stagnating, demanding to be broken down and made over.

It's worth remembering that if you resist the change advocated by this card, you might find that life imposes it upon you anyway.

Bottom Line Interpretations (Tarantino): Just when you think you have everything in order, it will change. Don't fight this reality. You may have to juggle your time, energy, and money to achieve your objectives. You don't have to take big steps, but small, consistent ones. Negative: you've become attached to a particular way of doing things thereby limiting the possibilities. Keep your sense of humor. Matters will improve the minute you see the changes as opportunities for expansion than problems to be dealt with.

Advice: Remember that change is the support of stability. Be alert for opportunities, flow with changes.

The card is especially strengthened by cards like Fortune, and positive Disks and Wands. You can usually track down which area of life it applies to by looking at the cards that surround it. Cups would suggest you need to look at your emotional life. Disks would imply that it's either working or financial area that needs attention. Swords would probably indicate conflict around whatever changes you need to make, and may point to a need for clear communication. Wands would be more connected with your own application of will, and the way you are trying to build your life. Major Arcana cards would suggest an inner, more spiritual area needs to be looked at.

THREE OF DISKS: WORKS

TAROTNYMS

Successful balance of thought (planning/vision), energy (will), and execution/focus (action) versus a need for same

Development/making it happen/accomplishment/starting new plans or are on the way versus stuck in the unlimited possibilities or brainstorming phase/being without direction

Stability/gradual progress versus a desire/need to establish a bulkhead against a sea of constant change/force

ELEMENTAL SNAPSHOT

THE METHOD FOR DEALING WITH LIFE (EARTHLY EFFORT)

MAIN SUMMARY MESSAGE:

Work, commercial transaction, business, constructive, increase of material things, growth, commencement of new projects. Can also indicate selfishness, narrowness, greediness.

SYMBOLISM:

- Zodiac = Capricorn (sign of the duty); Planet = Mars (Sign of aggression and power);
- The red wheels at the corners of the translucent pyramid represent the three Gunas of the Hindu system of air, fire, and earth, the forces that make the wheels turn. The pyramid is in balance indicating stable construction. The

pyramid is in an ocean (water/the eternal) from which visible forms emerge but are not the complete reality.

DIVINATION:

Indicates the full engagement of energy, ideas, and resources united in pursuit of common goal. Gradual progress follows hard work.

Bottom Line Interpretations (Tarantino): A stable period of success. When you commit your talents, skills, and resources, and work hard the world opens up, sending you the opportunities and support you need. Use your common sense, develop a down to earth approach to any obstacles, and attend to your day-to-day business. People are attracted to your strong sense of propriety and will have faith in you. Negative: you are not committing yourself, time or energy to matters at hand. Your initial enthusiasm may have caused you to underestimate what would be required to succeed. Unless you put everything on the line, things will not work out in your favor. Growth and expansion will not be found by trying to stay in a safe, comfortable space.

Advice: Hard work and concentration can eventually gain you your highest objectives. But it's important to remember that you need to be fully focused on the project in hand, allowing nothing to get in the way.

FOUR OF DISKS: POWER

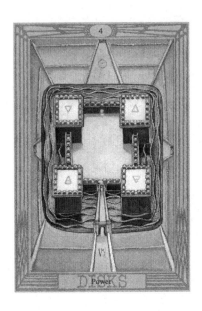

TAROTNYMS

Stability, structure, order and consistency have been achieved versus a change may be on the horizon/despite appearances, all is not as it seems

Security versus order-crushing creativity/trapped by current "safe" life

A successful model of reality has been constructed versus confusing our model with reality/becoming wedded to our view

ELEMENTAL SNAPSHOT

THE HOPE OF LIFE (EARTHLY STABILITY)

MAIN SUMMARY MESSAGE:

Power, law and order, gain of money and influence, success, rank, dominion. Can also mean envy, prejudice, and lack of originality.

SYMBOLISM:

- Zodiac = Capricorn (sign of duty); Planet = Sun (sign of pure energy);
- The disks are very large and solid, representing the four elements (fire, water, air, earth) suggesting a fortress (with a moat [the dark blue/black]). Law and order maintained by constant vigilance (the four squares contain symbols for the four elements, which are depicted as being in constant motion). Note that the pathway/bridge into the center is the only way in and narrow indicating control and choice of stability/safety/rules over creativity/uncertainty/risk. Revolution is the opposite of this card.

DIVINATION:

Represents the time when we achieve a stable level of material balance—at least for that moment in time. At the purely mundane level, it might come up after we had settled into a new home, or undertaken major improvements. The card is, at this level, much concerned with asset security and material bounty.

May indicate submission to a prescribed order that has both positive and negative effects. The person is someone one can depend on, remains true to their principles. At the same time, they may end up rigid sticklers, crusading for one's principles. Cold, stiff, politeness can replace real warmth and friendship.

Bottom Line Interpretations (Tarantino): Through structure, planning, and organization, you have achieved a strong foundation. Whatever you are considering, first consider what the ends results should look like. Next, list your resources. Third, draft a step-by-step plan. And finally, work backwards from the outcome to determine your first steps. Negative: you need to determine what you wish to achieve in the long run and then prioritize. Learn to say, "no," when appropriate. Through proper planning, discipline, and hard work, you can get what you want.

Advice: One thing to bear in mind when this card appears—though you have achieved one level of material stability, you cannot cling to this, or take it for granted. Become too smug and you'll find yourself losing the sense of safety and balance which has occurred. The human being is not naturally given to stagnation.

FIVE OF DISKS: WORRY

TAROTNYMS

Crisis/awareness and will to change versus pessimism/inner fear for which there is no obvious external solution/futile and senseless suffering

Uncertainty/transience of all life versus opportunity to change/grow

Security falters/risks taken become problematic/shaky foundation versus period of re-examination/re-appraisal/new insights/success around the corner

ELEMENTAL SNAPSHOT

THE ANXIETY OF LIFE (EARTHLY UNCERTAINTY)

MAIN SUMMARY MEANING:

Worry, intense strain, inactivity, financial loss, monetary anxiety, professional setbacks.

SYMBOLISM:

- Zodiac = Taurus (sign of strength, earthiness); Planet = Mercury (sign of will and swiftness);
- The card shows a disruption of the elements, the gears are turning but the inverted pentagram symbolizes feeling stuck. The card is bright yellow with red streaks trying to shine through indicating that things may look good from the outside but inside there is doubt and uncertainty. Red triangle, energy blocked; yellow, thoughts revolve around trying to find a solution;

blue crescent, cuts through you; black, a hole, no way out; blue circle, inner wisdom admonishes to do something.

DIVINATION:

All the 5's in the deck are demanding cards—the number five relates to the planet Mars, which can sometimes have a disruptive destructive energy. On the other hand though, Martian power, strength and determination are necessary attributes to break through obstacles and difficulties.

There looks to be financial, material or domestic trouble on the horizon. Something poses a threat to your overall security. This might be an unexpected expense, or job worries, or maybe even a disturbance in your family life. But there's one important thing to bear in mind—whatever is causing the problem is much more of a threat than it is a reality.

Bottom Line Interpretations (Tarantino): Worry is often a stage in the realization of one's dreams. You are leaving behind the security of the family and breaking down the structure and routine to which you've become accustomed. Keep the faith as you move through uncertainty and anxiety that accompanies a new endeavor. You will either restructure the foundation of or develop a totally different approach to your circumstances. Negative: all the worrying you've done hasn't helped and has, in fact, hindered your progress. Turn away from doubt. Success is on the horizon even if you can't yet see its light.

Advice: It is important not to feed that possibility with our own fear. Fear is a powerful emotion. It can rule if we let it. When this card comes up, remember that disturbance is possible—guaranteed. Do all you can to avert it.

SIX OF DISKS: SUCCESS

TAROTNYMS

Achievement of balance/security and stability in work, family, home, finances versus neglecting an important part of life necessary for balance

Material or personal gain/wishes fulfilled versus time to be charitable/share/be open for a new opportunity

Sense of happiness/atmospheric harmony versus awareness that change is constant/need to enjoy what one has or share/be tolerant/gracious

ELEMENTAL SNAPSHOT

THE ABUNDANCE OF LIFE (EARTHLY SUCCESS)

MAIN SUMMARY MEANING:

Success, material gain, power, influence, philanthropy. Can also mean conceit with wealth.

SYMBOLISM:

- Zodiac = Taurus (sign of strength, earthiness); Planet = Moon (inner, imagination, unconscious, reflective, illusive, emotion);
- The six disks are arranged in a hexagram (each bearing the symbol of a planet, balanced by another planet: Mars and Venus = War and Peace; Jupiter and Saturn = Abundance and Deprivation; Mercury and Jupiter = Doubt and Faith; Moon and Sun = Unconscious and Conscious), in the center the Sun as a rose (49 pedals) and cross, indicating a harmonious

establishment of energy in the element. Three concentric circles of warm colors, showing full realization of balance on earth.

DIVINATION:

Rather than interpreting Disks purely in a financial context, we are better served by seeing them as relating to the basic nuts and bolts of security. This includes money and finances, of course, but also covers all sorts of other areas too—the basic trust and reliability of our friends and family, the nature of our home, the set of tasks which form our job.

We have achieved a natural state of inner balance and harmony which allows us to use our energies without diversion or interference. More often than not, these energies are directed into practical channels—in the workplace, dealing with things in the home environment.

Bottom Line Interpretations (Tarantino): You are well on your way to success. Be prepared to accommodate the changes it will bring. Protect your sense of self-worth as all success is fleeting. Negative: it's easy to feel overwhelmed by matters at hand. Consider what you can do to make things more manageable. When you fall short, remember there's no such thing as failure, only results. If you are tenacious, you will succeed.

Advice: Take stock of your overall position in a practical sense. Use the abundance that comes to you, and be generous with your bounty. Ensure that others benefit appropriately from your abundance.

SEVEN OF DISKS: FAILURE

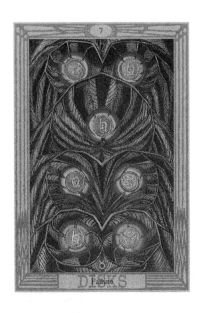

TAROTNYMS

Warning about current plans/not optimistic versus sober, down to earth appraisal and willingness to draw/face painful conclusions

Resignation/feeling limited or constrained versus keeping one's fears in check/breaking the problem down into small manageable pieces/keep one's feet moving

Lack or loss of security, fertility, creativity, hope versus warning to be aware/take one's time

ELEMENTAL SNAPSHOT

THE DEGENERATION OF LIFE (EARTHLY UPSETS)

MAIN SUMMARY MEANING:

Failure, enfeeblement, sickness, withering, blight.

SYMBOLISM:

- Zodiac = Taurus (sign of strength, earthiness); Planet = Saturn (slow, heavy, obstinate);
- The disks are leaden indicating bad money. They are also arranged in a geomantic figure—rubeus—an overturned glass. The vegetation in the background is overgrown and spoiled. Saturn requires discipline and structure. Taurus requires tenacity and hard work;

- The background looks like peacock feathers suggesting that fears and dread may belong more to the mental plane, than physical reality.

DIVINATION:

This card marks the turn of the tide in both material and interpersonal matters. In a sense, card 7, Failure, marks the fullest possible establishment of matter (everything passes).

Generally the card will come up to mark a difficult period in material life. That job you went after probably won't be offered to you; your bank balance is giving you problems; you don't seem to be able to get on top of things no matter how you try; unexpected bills turn up, causing you worry.

You see insurmountable obstacles. If you find yourself having a real run of bad financial fortune, it's time to examine your own reactions to making a success of yourself. If you believe you'll fail, then you surely will. If you allow fears about money and security to dominate your experience, then everything will be darkened by your own expectations.

Bottom Line Interpretations (Tarantino): You've convinced yourself that you can't possibly succeed. However, success is not a goal in itself, it's a state of mind. Examine the reasons for your current evaluation to determine whether they are a matter of objective reality or your ideas and beliefs about what constitutes success. Negative: your attitude about success and failure is changing. It's time to take control of your life. There are seven steps: envision your goal, imagine yourself living your dream, compare your present circumstance to your values, let your passion motivate you, small steps, develop a network of support, and do it.

Advice: The solution is to see things from a different point of view. By affirming the positive things that we do for ourselves in the material sphere, we will improve that area of our lives—this is true of any area. So even when things are looking very black, it's important to try to keep our fears under control, and to bear in mind that what we give out is what we get back. Re-examine our personal attitudes about finances, material success and security when this card comes up.

If it appears to mark a time where we are in financial difficulties, we must first look at what we're REALLY thinking. Remember, what you put your attention on grows bigger. So instead you have to, by an effort of deliberate will, put your attention on your income, upon the funds you have available to you.

EIGHT OF DISKS: PRUDENCE

TAROTNYMS

Solid planning, loving execution and attention bears fruit/recognition of connections and details versus lack of freedom/creativity/carried away by surrounding chaos

Thrifty/avoidance of excesses versus missed opportunities if "pound foolish"

Organized/practice/self-discipline versus spontaneous/natural beauty/ Stepford Wives

Turn in the tide of affairs/leaving the past behind versus patience while matters mature

ELEMENTAL SNAPSHOT

THE POWER OF PLANNING IN LIFE (EARTHLY FORESIGHT)

MAIN SUMMARY MEANING:

Prudence, intelligence in material affairs, agriculture, building, skill, cunning. Can also mean "penny wise and pound foolish."

SYMBOLISM:

- Zodiac = Virgo (details, organization); Planet = Sun (pure energy);
- The disks are arranged as the fruit of a great tree, (a geomantic figure—populous—indicating that the outcome is based on the people in the situation, or represents a large number of people or peers), its solid roots in

fertile ground, denoting intelligence lovingly applied to material matters. There are 8 dark pink flowers, each protected by a large leaf representing planning, forethought, and caution. The number 8 symbolizes harmony, adjustment, balance (card VIII, Adjustment). The blue, green, and yellow are favorable colors.

DIVINATION:

The 8 of disks implies the successful use skill, prudence, and cunning in labor. There is an implication here of being over-careful in small things at the expense of great. Be alert for opportunities, ready to deal with stress and pressure, and to manage your energies thoughtfully and carefully.

Bottom Line Interpretations (Tarantino): Anything worth doing is worth doing well. Do what needs to be done on a day-to-day basis, planning carefully and avoiding extremes. Be patient. Allow matters to develop at their own pace. Negative: take stock of the situation at hand. Your impatience for results may be getting in the way, tempting you to quit too soon. Just waiting won't help either. Be consistent and do not procrastinate. Do what needs to be done every day.

Advice: Extremes and excesses should be avoided. Every bloom on a tree is protected by a large leaf. Also, remember, the tree is just beginning to bear fruit. It's not time for harvesting or giving out newly developing wealth.

Be alert for opportunities, but manage your energies thoughtfully and carefully. Be aware of the correlation which exists with regard to energy management between the material and spiritual definitions of the card—in either case energy must be regulated and respected in order for life to go smoothly and for you to get the best out of your experiences. If beginning a new undertaking, insure that health and finances are enough to allow for success.

NINE OF DISKS: GAIN

TAROTNYMS

Success, promotion, advancement versus struggling to achieve success

Sense of growth and fulfillment following much work and investment versus needing to work hard to achieve growth and fulfillment

Inner happiness versus resolution of an ongoing conflict on the horizon

ELEMENTAL SNAPSHOT

INCREASE/GROWTH IN LIFE (EARTHLY ADVANCE)

MAIN SUMMARY MEANING:

Gain (due to hard work), favor, popularity, growth. Material benefits abound.

SYMBOLISM:

- Zodiac = Virgo (sign of details and organization); Planet = Venus (love and beauty);

- The disks are arranged in an equilateral triangle of three (love, creativity, wisdom), apex upward, surrounded by a ring. Six disks form a hexagon, symbolizing the good luck attending material affairs (the combination of karma, ambition and ability, love and devotion). The tip of the top triangle points up, corresponding to the fire element, and down in the bottom triangle, symbolizing water. The faces of Crowley (the developer), Lady Harris (the artist), and Israel Regardie (Crowley's personal assistant) are pictured on the six disks, their faces overlaid with the same 6 symbols of the planets found of the 6 of disks (Success) card;

- The background stands for earth water (green), air (blue), in the middle, the sun (fire).

DIVINATION:

At the mundane level it indicates the financial rewards which come from working diligently and dedicatedly on an important project, so it will often mark a stage of completion.

Sometimes the card indicates consolidation and achievement at home. Perhaps an emotional conflict has finally been resolved, or a long-standing problem finally dealt with.

At the spiritual level, this card talks a lot about the principle that what we give to life is what we get back. And here we have confirmation that we have lived as much as we are able in the moment, appreciating the things that come our way, and celebrating the bounty we have. As a result, more abundance flows in.

The card rarely indicates windfalls, or unexpected sources of income. Here we have worked hard to create something rewarding, and the Gain card indicates the results of our efforts.

Bottom Line Interpretations (Tarantino): The seeds you've planted will soon blossom. Take time now to address any unfinished business, however insignificant it may seem. Your success will extend to your relationships, career, and general well-being. Take time to appreciate it. Such feelings will allow you to envision new dreams using the blueprint you've established. Negative: the lack of progress is wearing you down. You are under no obligation to do anything you don't want to do. Success will be difficult if your heart isn't in it. If you don't want to commit completely, you might as well cut your losses and get out.

Advice: That phrase "what goes around comes around" is very relevant to this card. Be open to opportunities which allow us to conclude work that has been outstanding; remain alert to new chances opening up before us. This card accords with the ancient wisdom that we give what we get in life—so this is also a day to look for opportunities to offer our help and resources with no immediate expectation of return.

TEN OF DISKS: WEALTH

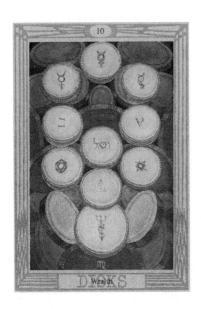

TAROTNYMS

The results of one's efforts/completion of one's goals/reaching the pinnacle/being harvested versus the end of a cycle/need for new objectives

Prosperity/generosity versus greed/avarice

Happiness and harmony versus coming instability/need to prepare for change/nothing lasts forever

ELEMENTAL SNAPSHOTS

AFFLUENCE IN LIFE (EARTHLY RESULTS)

MAIN SUMMARY MEANING:

Wealth in financial, as well as spiritual, emotional, and relational matters. Happiness.

SYMBOLISM:

- Zodiac = Virgo (details and organization); Planet = Mercury (will and swiftness);

- The number 10 always represents the final issue of energy. Here is the great and final solidification. The force is completely expended and results in death;

- The disks have become coins, and are arranged in the Tree of Life, indicating that true wealth must touch all levels of life. The 10th is larger symbolizing the futility of material gain.

DIVINATION:

When we have created sufficient wealth to make ourselves comfortable and contented, if we have a surplus, then we must make that surplus work. We cannot expect energy to flow freely in our lives if we hoard it, and try to hang on to it. As you spread your wealth, the energy regenerates and returns to you tenfold.

Bottom Line Interpretations (Tarantino): It's not the money, love, or acclaim that matters but how you feel about these things that makes you wealthy. When you are fully able to enjoy the abundance already present in your life, more prosperity is likely to follow. Share your good fortune with others. Negative: scarcity is a major issue in your life at present. Open your mind to the abundance that surrounds you. Be prepared to look in a new direction for the fulfillment you seek.

Advice: Often, commentaries on this card warn that once sufficient wealth has been attained, you should make sure you distribute excess fairly and generously. This is because energy which remains unused eventually corrupts and dissipates.

But there's another aspect to the right use of energy which is not so often addressed. This is to do with the way the will works. There's a common misunderstanding about the use of will among us—we tend to think that applying will is something that we only do consciously. This is incorrect. The human will works all the time. It runs around happily creating whatever seems most pressing in your mind.

This has a rather unfortunate side effect. For many people, the most pressing emotions and responses in their minds are connected to fear, pain, unhappiness or deprivation. All the time that cycle is taking place, your will is wildly scampering after all those negative feelings and channeling your energy out into life, attempting to create the things it thinks you want. By bringing our thoughts and emotions to a conscious level, and by making positive choices about how we direct those energies, we create our world. So we need to decide what we want, and then think about that, not linger on the things that we don't want.

KNIGHT OF DISKS

TAROTNYMS

Hard work finished/battle won/time to harvest/properly done job versus caught up in petty matters/or short versus long sighted/half done

Down to earth/pragmatic versus lacking inspiration/dogmatic

Tenacious versus authoritarian/controlling/self-absorbed

Constancy/action guided by sober assessment versus lack of creativity

Time for a well-deserved rest versus pushing ahead/failing to take time for inspiration or consolidation/enjoying what one has

ELEMENTAL SNAPSHOT

THE FATHER OF THE HARVEST (EARTHLY REWARD)

MAIN SUMMARY MESSAGE:

The fiery part of earth. Harvester, healer, toil as well as abundance. Endurance. Inclination toward convention, stability, and hard work. Success comes from hard work and earthly instincts not through abstract intellect. Ill-dignified can indicate someone so caught up in earthly matters (materialistic) that they are incapable of foresight into their own affairs or taking an intellectual interest in anything outside themselves.

SYMBOLISM:

- Zodiac = Virgo (details and organization);
- Element = Earth;
- Wheat fields indicate that it is harvest time, the grain is ripe;
- Clothed as a warrior, and his helmet is crested with a stag, indicative of preoccupation with the material world;
- He is armed with a flail pointed at the ground representing planting and harvesting;
- Mounted on a shire horse who has all four legs firmly planted on the ground (unlike the other Knights), symbolic of stability, structure, tradition. The horse is exhausted from hard work;
- The knight restricted in heavy armor indicative of someone enslaved in earthly matters;
- The stag's head on the visor indicates enhanced perception;
- The disk shows understanding of the physical plane. The concentric circles emanating from the shield (a disk representing nutrition) transform the brown hills in the background to green;
- Brown symbolizes earth, stability, fertility; green creativity, growth, healing; golden yellow, sun for crops.

It's not easy to take the fire of one's passion and materialize it. It takes hard work and commitment.

DIVINATION:

The freedom the spirit seeks will not be found in fleeing earthly realities. Freedom develops through surrender, with love and service, to all earthly dimension of life.

The tasks ahead are large and demand the use of all your power. Follow through and you will reap the harvest.

Bottom Line Interpretations (Tarantino): A time of harvest is at hand. In the meantime, you must continue to maintain a practical approach. It is not enough to have great ideas. You also need a well-structured plan in place. This is not a good time for innovative maneuvers. For now, follow a well-worn path. Pay attention to details. Stop and fix things that are out of place before continuing. There's no need to run around unnecessarily. When it is the right time, everything will fall into place. Negative: lately, you've been spreading yourself too thin. Consider focusing all your effort in one direction. Come down to earth, develop roots to sustain and support you going forward. Sober regard and perseverance will pay off.

Advice: Now is the time to take charge and address challenges head on. Stop being absorbed by petty matters

QUEEN OF DISKS

TAROTNYMS

Growth and stamina/hard working/ creative (especially in family matters) versus no time for self/risk of exploitation/emotional

Good instincts/life experience/ practical versus quiet/timid

Able to set boundaries and assert herself/confident yet sensible versus passive/lonely

An oasis in the desert/one of a kind/ wise in matters of family, economics, practical matters versus never in the forefront/not given credit/taken for granted

ELEMENTAL SNAPSHOT

THE MOTHER OF GROWTH (EARTHLY RESOURCE)

MAIN SUMMARY MEANING:

The watery part of earth, or fertility. An ambitious woman, yet affectionate and kind, charming, timid, practical, quiet and domesticated. Can also be foolish, capricious and moody.

SYMBOLISM:

- Zodiac = Capricorn;
- Element = Earth;

- On a throne, amid vegetation, symbolizing natural abundance and prosperity;
- The barren desert symbolizes the past, the challenges she has gone through to arrive at understanding. The river flowing through the desert is a thread she has followed;
- Crowned with spiral horns symbolizing her instincts perceptiveness;
- Her scepter is topped with a cube/hexagram indicting that she sees is clear about what she is doing and why (motives);
- Disk of circles and loops, along with her chest armor and skirt of coins, represents the physical world and her understanding of it (it is "in her hands");
- The goat on the sphere symbolizes stubbornness, tenacity, go her own way.

DIVINATION:

People typified by this card possess the finest of the quieter qualities. They are ambitious but only in useful directions. They possess immense funds of affection, kindness, and greatness of heart. They are not intellectual. They are quiet, hardworking, practical, and sensible.

A person whose attention centers upon the family environment. Here, she will excel, gaining a great deal of pleasure from providing a secure haven where she and others can feel cosseted and cared for. The risk is she can lose sight of her position—or, perhaps, is being taken for granted by others. At that point the weaker side of her personality will show through. She may become dependent and clingy, believing herself to be unable to stand alone. She might manipulate by adopting a passive victim's role.

Bottom Line Interpretations (Tarantino): The dry spell is over. You are about to or have just arrived at an oasis. This is a time to be cool, clam, and collected. You've done your job. Matters must now be allowed to evolve in their own way and at their own pace. Nurture. Act only when you can influence the outcome. Negative: its easy to get caught up in the struggle and hardship of life and miss the abundant joy and pleasure available. Consider that matters have changed. Don't quit simply because the results aren't materializing as quickly as you wanted.

Advice: The key here is to spend time and energy both on yourself, and your home—and to do both of these things with the intent to harmonize more thoroughly, to feel more rested and centered, to make more of a haven than we already have.

PRINCE OF DISKS

TAROTNYMS

Open, trusting (and trustworthy) versus naïve

Purposeful, driven, goal-focused versus needing to figure out one's goals, create a plan, and take matters step by step

Diligent, industrious/an "old soul" versus unemotional/perhaps unsympathetic

Creating the world one wants to live in/belief that he can do anything he puts his mind and effort to versus lack of pleasure/enjoying the moment

ELEMENTAL SNAPSHOT

THE SON OF LIFE (EARTHLY DETERMINATION)

MAIN SUMMARY MEANING:

The airy part of earth. Energetic with practical matters, steadfast, enduring, competent, skeptical of spirituality yet open, slow to anger, almost lacking in emotions.

SYMBOLISM:

- Zodiac = Taurus;
- Element = Eaerth;
- Seated in a chariot drawn by a bull symbolizing unfailing will and determination to reach his goal;

- He is naked, symbolizing openness, making him trustworthy to others;
- The disk resembles a globe with mathematical symbols indicating planning and practicality;
- The tapestry symbolizes the abundance of Earth and his determination to surround itself with its beauty; relatedly, the scepter with globe and cross, indicate that this determination is a crusade;
- Seedpods represent growth.

DIVINATION:

An unfailing determination to reach his goals, achieve his ambitions and create a world he is comfortable to live in. He has an interesting way of doing this—he takes every task a stage at a time. While keeping the end aim in mind, he diligently attends to the task in hand, completing it satisfactorily and then moving on smoothly to the next logical stage.

His approach to life overall is one of industrious practicality. He believes that all things yield to a determined will and well-directed activity. A quiet and meditative man, who works with unfailing determination towards the goals he sets himself. He is reliable and resourceful, unswerving and creative in his dedication.

He is more imaginative than the Knight of Disks, though he has the same quiet strength and gentleness. His quality of contemplation often yields fruit in surprising ways, generating a deep and broad-sweeping understanding about the inner workings of life.

Bottom Line Interpretations (Tarantino): Convention and practicality are called for. Leave emotion out of it. Adopt a conservative approach. Although it may seem unchallenging, now is the time to operate from a well-developed plan with clear-cut goals. Allow others to think you are making concessions. Negative: you're vacillating between manic activity and lethargy. Don't expect quick results. Matters will take time to unfold and materialize. Learn everything you can. Remain objective. Stick to the tried and true.

Advice: Take everything a stage at a time. Decide early on what you're actually hoping to achieve during the day—and make this a reachable goal. Then plot your method of working toward it.

PRINCESS OF DISKS

TAROTNYM

New growth, big changes, new beginnings, germination of life or opportunities for same (finances and home especially) versus needing to be prepared for possibility of same

Marriage, union, fusion or drive for same for creative purposes versus needing to (or now is the time to) express one's self creatively (following long preparation)/let one's self become animated/inspired

Possibility of a warm, sensual bond versus hedonism, indolence, sentimentality

ELEMENTAL SNAPSHOT

THE DAUGHTER OF MOTHER EARTH (EARTHLY CREATIVITY)

MAIN SUMMARY MEANING:

The earthy part of earth. Strong, beautiful, generous, brooding. Womanhood in its ultimate projection. Giving birth to all possibilities.

SYMBOLISM:

- Element = Earth;
- A young woman, beautiful and strong, pregnant with possibilities. This is the third card in the tarot associated with motherhood (The Empress, Queen of

Cups). She is generous, kind, diligent, benevolent. Her headdress with ram indicate strength and determination to bring her vision to reality. The braids in her long red (integrity, clear perception) hair symbolize three beings, mother, child, and father. Her animal skin cape symbolizes human instincts;

- In the disk, the Chinese ideogram (yin/yang) denoting the twin spiral force of creation in equilibrium, balance between receptive and active nature;
- The scepter with crystal pointed at the ground represents the ability to make a reality out of her intentions;
- The wheat stalks on the altar symbolize prosperity, abundance;
- The earth tones represent grounding and sacred, yellow spirit.

DIVINATION:

A reliable and diligent person, trustworthy and hard-working. She is faithful by nature, and deals badly with conflict. She likes life to unfold in an ordered fashion. In fact, she contemplates life very thoroughly, being sensitive to the needs of others, and sympathetic to their feelings.

Despite her quiet exterior, she has a huge resource of strength and support to offer to those who need it. She is also an excellent practical manager with marked proficiency in dealing with money and accounting. This will, however, generally be expressed in the home environment where she is at her most content. Something new is about to enter the person's life.

This card is one with a great deal of hidden strength and power within it, which promises new growth, big changes and new beginnings, accompanied by the inner reserves to make the best of those influences.

A day ruled by this Princess is one on which financial matters will usually work well, and where you may quite possibly receive good news regarding money and wealth.

Bottom Line Interpretations (Tarantino): You are capable of turning your dreams into reality. Don't allow your native energy to be dampened by the dull, routine work you have to do. Take your time and don't hurry. Go slowly, and be methodical. Negative: you've spent a lot of time dreaming about this venture but your present circumstances have left you feeling emotionally drained and lethargic. Do what you need to do to restore your energy and sense of well-being, including a change of scenery.

Advice: Pay special attention to ideas you have during a day like this, and be prepared to think them through and act on them as soon as the time is right.

BIBLIOGRAPHY

Akron, and Banzhaf, H. (1995). *The Crowley Tarot: The Handbook to the Cards.* Stamford, CT: US Games.

Aleister Crowley's Thoth Tarot: An Instruction Booklet by the Hermit. http://tarotcrowley.blogspot.com/search/label/Twos

Angel Paths. http://www.angelpaths.com/about.html

B.O.T.A. in Europe: A Mystery School. http://www.botaineurope.org/index.php?id=16

Crowley, A. (2013). *The Book of Thoth (Egyptian Tarot).* San Francisco, CA: Weiser Books.

Fairchild, D. (1999). *Tarot.* Philadelphia, PA: Running Press.

Grossberg, S. (2008). *Bauta "Hiding Place" Quadrant (Scott Grossberg): Betraying the Face of Illusion.* Orlando, FL: Leaping Lizards Magic.

Heidrick, B. (1989). Tarot Correspondence Tables. http://www.billheidrick.com/works/tarottbl.htm

Hughes-Barlow, P. A *Compendium of Tarot Card Meanings.* http://supertarot.co.uk/meaning/tarotcardmeanings.htm

Pyreaus: Divination, Mythology, Discovery. http://www.pyreaus.com

Raven's Tarot Site. http://www.corax.com/tarot

Tarantino, P.C. (2007). *Tarot for the New Aeon.* Pebble Beach, CA: Alternative Publishing.

Tarot Eon: A Tarot Blog. http://taroteon.com/tarot-lexicon/four-things-you-need-to-know-about-the-fool/

Wasserman, J. (1983). *Instructions for Aleister Crowley's Thoth Tarot Deck.* Stamford, CT: US Games.

Wasserman, J. (2006). *Aleister Crowley's Thoth Tarot Deck* (Edited and Updated by Lynn Araujo). Stamford, CT: US Games.

Webster, R. (2012). *The Tarot for Fun and Profit* (New Edition). Auckland, New Zealand: Brookfield Press.

Ziegler, G. (1988). *Tarot: Mirror of the Soul.* San Francisco, CA: Weiser Books.

Made in the USA
San Bernardino, CA
09 April 2020